HOW TO RESEARCH YOUR GERMAN ANCESTORS

HOW TO RESEARCH YOUR GERMAN ANCESTORS

by
PETER TOWEY
Vice-President, Anglo-German Family History Society

3rd Edition (2013)

ANGLO-GERMAN FAMILY HISTORY SOCIETY PUBLICATIONS

© Copyright 2013 Peter Towey and Anglo German Family History Society 2013.

All rights reserved.
No part of this publication may be reproduced in
any form without prior permission from the publisher.

First published by the Federation of Family History Societies (FFHS) as *An Introduction to Tracing Your German Ancestors*, by Peter Towey, in 1998.

Second edition, 2002.

ISBN 978-0-9571763-0-0

British Library and cataloguing data
A catalogue record of this book is available from the British Library.

Designed originated by Rochart and printed on paper sourced from sustainable forests by MWL Digital, Wales.

Contents

Introduction	7
PART I: Tracing German Ancestors in Great Britain	10
An overview of the history of German Immigration	10
Using British Records:	11
The Censuses	11
Naturalization and Denization	12
Records of Aliens	17
German Churches in the UK	17
Jewish Records	27
Records of the British Armed Services	28
The Merchant Navy	33
Hon. East India Company	34
The City of London	35
Immigration Records	35
German Occupations	38
Internment	44
If you still do not know where they came from...	49
Names	49
Telephone Directories	50
Genealogical Dictionaries	51
Coats of Arms (Wappen)	53
Auswanderer or German Emigrant records	54
German Passenger Lists	56
PART II: Tracing German Ancestors in the German-speaking parts of Europe	58
German Historical Geography	59
Records Microfilmed by the LDS Church	62
The German Alphabet	62
Civil Registration	63
Church Registers	70
Wills	74
Censuses	74
Military and Naval Records	76

Registration of Inhabitants (Einwohnermelde)	81
Burger Lists or Books	82
Address Books or Directories	82
Dorfsippenbücher, Ortssippenbücher & Ortsfamilienbücher	83
The former German territories in Eastern Europe	84
Advice on individual parts of Germany	88
States outside the German Empire with significant	
German-Speaking Populations	96
The Austro-Hungarian Empire	96
The Russian Empire	100
Switzerland	102
Abbreviations	103
Index	104

Introduction

My book on researching your German ancestors has now been out of print for several years. Many of you have been kind enough to urge me to update and republish it. Since it was first published by the Federation of Family History Societies in 1998 a lot has changed. The Internet in particular has radically altered research methods and has made research in many parts of Germany easier. I have therefore decided, while keeping the general pattern of the book, which many of you have found helpful, to revise the contents completely. To those of you who are still wary of using the Internet, I do apologise but it does make so much difference to researchers that I have to build this book around it rather than just append an additional chapter. In most parts of the UK, if you do not have a computer connected to the Internet at home, you can use one at your local public library. Wherever possible, however, I have made an effort to include information that will help the Internet-averse.

As you have opened this book, you may know that you have German ancestors. Some will even know who they were and where they came from. Many of you, however, will only suspect that the family's surname looks "German" or will know that an ancestor came from Germany but not where or when. This book aims to help all of you.

First of all, however, it is necessary to define what we mean by "German". There was no State called Germany until 1871. Before then there was a multiplicity of sovereign Kingdoms (eg Prussia, Bavaria, Saxony, Württemberg, Austria); Grand Dukedoms (eg Hesse, Baden); Dukedoms (eg Brunswick); many smaller states like Schaumburg-Lippe or Saxe-Coburg-Gotha, and even free city states like Hamburg, Frankfurt am Main and Bremen. The relationships of these states to each other, their boundaries and even their names and existence varied over time. The importance of this for the family historian is that each state kept its own records and had different laws about what needed to be recorded. Unlike England and Wales or Scotland there is no single place where all the records can be consulted. Even after Civil Registration covered the whole of pre First World War Germany in 1876, the records were not centralised but were usually kept in the local town hall. To do research in Germany, therefore, you need a good atlas! I intend, therefore, to deal in this book with the German-speaking parts of Europe including Austria as well as the territories in the East that now form parts of Poland, the Ukraine and Russia; any part of this vast area could have been called "Germany" in the recent past.

Anyone who believes that they have German ancestry in the UK is urged to join the Anglo-German Family History Society. The Society was formed in 1987 by several British family historians who had discovered that they had German roots but had no idea how to research them. Since then it has sought out, indexed and, in some cases, published records that are likely to inform and help others in the same position. It has also published books on aspects of German life in the United Kingdom: on internment, on the German churches, and on sugar bakers, pork butchers, hairdressers and other German occupations. If you are new to German research, someone in the Society has probably been there before you and should be able to advise. The quarterly magazine, "Mitteilungsblatt", contains articles on many aspects of research and its index is well worth a look. I should add that, despite its name, the magazine is in English!

The Society does not have offices but is run by volunteers from their homes. It holds meetings on Saturdays in London six times a year: February, April, June (including the AGM), August, October and December. From time to time members organize meetings locally in their area which can be helpful for members who cannot easily get to London. Full details of the meetings are available online at the Society's website **www.agfhs.org.uk**. The Society also has pages on **www.genfair.com** which is an online bookshop from which you can purchase their publications.

The Society has, over the years, built up a large computerised *Name Index* which currently contains well over 500,000 entries, principally of Germans in the UK. The sources used are various including most of the church registers of the German churches in England and Scotland; the records of the King's German Legion; many Aliens' records from TNA, and many other miscellaneous sources. It includes all the indexes which Len Metzner compiled over the years, the sources for which are listed in *Catalogue of Len Metzner Indexes*, published by Anglo-German FHS in 2000. This Index is not online and is only available for use by members of the Society but, as you can imagine, is well worth a search.

It is also worth recording that the Library of the Society of Genealogists in London contains an excellent and growing collection of books that will be of great help to anyone researching their German ancestry. It is the best collection of such books available anywhere in the UK.

This book is divided into two parts: Part I deals with finding where in Germany or the German-speaking parts of Europe your immigrant ancestor came from and Part II deals with researching in the German-speaking parts of Europe. As it is quite impossible to do more than scratch the surface in a book of this size, I have incorporated details of books and other material that you can use to take it further.

I would like to take this opportunity of thanking all those who have helped me in putting this book together. I would like to acknowledge the assistance of the staff of The National Archives and London Metropolitan Archives for their help with their records; the members of the Anglo-German FHS who have taught me so much about German family history over the last 25 years; but, in particular, Roy Bernard, and his late wife, Margaret, for founding the Anglo-German FHS and nurturing it over its first decade; Len Metzner and the late Pam Freeman for giving so much of their time to tracking down, preserving and indexing records of Germans in UK; and Jenny Towey, my wife, and the Society's Secretary for its first 11 years, for encouraging me to update this book and putting up with me while I did so!

Peter Towey, Plymouth, Devon, May 2013

PART I:
Tracing German Ancestors in Great Britain

A short overview of the history of German Immigration

There have been Germans living in Great Britain, particularly London, since the beginning of our recorded history. Germany was, after all, only on the other side of the North Sea. When the thrones of Great Britain and Hanover were united in the person of King George I in 1714 many Hanoverians came with him and since then there has been a constant stream of German-speaking immigrants.

The records of the Army, Royal Navy and Royal Marines and even the East India Company testify to the numbers of young German men seeking their fortune in the British services. Many German princelings made their budgets balance by selling the regiments they raised into British service – the "Hessians" who fought for King George III in the American War of Independence are the best known but there were many others. During the French Revolutionary and Napoleonic Wars many more young men fled the invading French armies and took ship to England. Some trying to escape being pressed into Napoleon's Armies ended up being pressed into the British Army or Navy! A whole army, the Hanoverian army, escaped and served in the British Army as the King's German Legion until Hanover was freed and the troops were able to go home in 1814.

In the 19th century the flow of immigrants from the German states increased. It is estimated that by the 1840s some 30,000 Germans were living in England, making up by far the largest immigrant community. Many of them lived and worked in poor conditions in the East End of London.

After the failure of the 1848 democratic revolt in Germany, many academics and other middle class Germans came to London – many settling in Camberwell in Surrey. Rosemary Ashton's book, *Little Germany. Exile and Asylum in Victorian England*, OUP, 1986, looks at the experiences of the 1848 refugees in England.

But the main influx from the beginning of the 19th century was of young Germans seeking their fortune in the main industrialized power of the age and, especially, in the capital of the British Empire: London. This influx continued until the outbreak of the First World War in 1914. In the run up to and during the War people with Germanic names and Germanic accents were subject to hatred and mob violence and, after the Lusitania was sunk in 1915, German males of fighting age who had not become naturalized British citizens were interned. During and after the War many German nationals were forcibly repatriated and this really was the end of the pre-War German community. Because of their treatment in the War, many British people of German descent changed their names and tried to bury all trace of their German descent; in many cases they were all too successful and their descendants often do not realise that they have German ancestry until they start researching.

Using British Records

Just because you have found an ancestor with a German name, it does not mean that he or she was born in Germany; my great great grandfather Wernint Weyman was actually born in Whitechapel in 1822. It was his father, Johann Friedrich Weyman, who was the immigrant. So you need to trace your ancestry through British records in the usual way until you find which one was an immigrant.

The Censuses
The most usual way of discovering this in 19th century records is from the censuses. From 1851 onwards, the enumerator was required to record the birthplace of each individual. Sadly it was considered that the name of the Country of birth was enough if outside England and Wales so you often only find "Germany" or "Prussia" or "Hanover" in the "Where Born" column. Sometimes though you can be lucky and get the name of the village or town. That is why it is even more essential than usual to trace your possibly-German ancestor through each of the censuses: 1851, 1861,

1871, 1881, 1891, 1901 and 1911 – if the birthplace is given in just one of the censuses it will save you a great deal of searching.

The 1841 census does not even give the Country of birth for immigrants but puts an "F" in the "Where Born" column meaning "born in Foreign Parts". This is better than nothing, however, as it is an indication that the person concerned was the immigrant. My Johann Friedrich Weyman, by then known by the very English-looking name of Frederick Weyman died in 1847 and it was only when I found him in the 1841 census that I realized that he was born a foreigner. His son, baptised Wernint Weyman at St Mary, Whitechapel, was subsequently known as William Weyman – to all appearances just as English as his father.

As with most records, it is not always clear exactly what the placename recorded in the "Where born" column in the census actually means. Does "Hanover" mean the city or the Kingdom? What does "Germany" mean before 1871? Does "Germany, British Subject" mean that the individual had become a naturalized British Subject since being born in Germany or that they were the child of British subjects and just happened to be born in Germany? Even when you know what the description ought to have meant, how sure are you that the enumerator knew or cared? In many cases individuals noted as "Nat BS" (or "Naturalized British Subject") in a census do not appear to have been naturalized at all. Probably the immigrant, possibly with poor English, did not understand the census question and thought he was being asked if he was a loyal subject of the Queen.

Naturalization and Denization

The obvious records to go to, if you believe your ancestor was an immigrant, are the Home Office records at the National Archives (TNA) at Kew. Their website is **www.nationalarchives.gov.uk**.

The National Archives' new online catalogue, Discovery, indexes the Naturalization Certificates (from 1870) and the relevant Home Office files, for each of the persons naturalized since the system of applying to the Home Office was adopted in 1844. When you input the name of the person you are researching in the search engine you will, hopefully, find a number of possible references. If the person was naturalized you should find two entries; one for the copy certificate (after 1870) and one for the Home Office file. The latter is more helpful as it will include the person's

British Nationality and Status of Aliens Act, 1914.

CERTIFICATE OF NATURALIZATION.

Whereas **Charles Frederick Seitz,**

has applied for a Certificate of Naturalization, alleging with respect to **him** the particulars set out below, and has satisfied me that the conditions laid down in the above-mentioned Act for the grant of a Certificate of Naturalization are fulfilled in **his** case

Now, therefore, in pursuance of the powers conferred on me by the said Act, I grant to the said **Charles Frederick Seitz,** this Certificate of Naturalization, and declare that upon taking the Oath of Allegiance within the time and in the manner required by the regulations made in that behalf **he** shall, subject to the provisions of the said Act, be entitled to all political and other rights powers and privileges, and be subject to all obligations duties and liabilities, to which a natural-born British subject is entitled or subject, and have to all intents and purposes the status of a natural-born British subject.

In witness whereof I have hereto subscribed my name this **20th** day of **August, 1923.**

W. C. BRIDGEMAN

HOME OFFICE,
    LONDON.

One of His Majesty's Principal Secretaries of State.

PARTICULARS RELATING TO APPLICANT.

Full Name	**Charles Frederick Seitz.**
Address	**17, Brunton Terrace, Sunderland.**
Trade or occupation	**Pork Butcher.**
Place and date of birth	**Hohebach, Wurtemberg, Germany.**
	15th July, 1878.
Nationality	**Of No Nationality.**
Married, single, widower, or widow	**Married.**
Name of wife, or husband	**Sarah.**
Names and nationality of parents	**John Andrew and Magdalene Margaret Dorothea Seitz. German.**

(FOR OATH *see overleaf.*)

Example of first page of a naturalization certificate.

application form, with his or her signature, a police or MI5 (depending on the period) report on the person – positive because otherwise they would not have been naturalized! Using the reference you can then order a copy of the papers on the file. I would advise against asking the TNA to organize the copying for you as it can be extremely expensive; employ a local researcher in London or go and do it yourself.

Also included in Discovery are naturalizations issued overseas between 1915 and 1982.

As a rough guide, "Denization" is a cheaper form of naturalization; the Denizen could purchase land but not inherit it, vote or hold public office; a Naturalized Subject had all the rights of someone born a British Subject. Denization ceased to be available as an option in 1873.

The best initial guide to naturalization and denization, however, is TNA's guide "Naturalization and British Citizenship" available online under their "Records" and "Looking for a Subject" headings. It outlines the complex history of citizenship and naturalization in the UK and tells you where you need to look for any records.

Until the First World War there was no legal requirement that aliens living in the United Kingdom must become naturalized. Many, indeed most, German and other aliens lived and died in the UK without naturalizing. Naturalization was an expensive business and for many there seemed to be no point. This was one of the reasons why so many who had lived in the UK for virtually all their lives were interned in the First World War and why they were so hurt and shocked by that treatment. The naturalization or denization records can be so helpful that it is always worth looking. However, German and other foreign women who married a British Subject automatically became a British Subject themselves until the latter part of the 20th Century. In those cases there will be no record of that woman becoming British other than the ordinary marriage certificate.

Before 1800
The indexes to Denizations and Naturalizations in England, Scotland, Wales and Ireland before 1800 are handily available in the published volumes of the Quarto Series of the Huguenot Society of Great Britain and Ireland and available in most large reference libraries and now available on CD: *Letters of Denization and Acts of Naturalization for Aliens*

in England, 1509-1603, (ed. William Page, publ. Huguenot Society of London, Quarto Series, vol. 8, 1893.) *Letters of Denization and Acts of Naturalization for Aliens in England and Ireland, 1603-1700*, (ed. William A. Shaw, publ. Huguenot Society of London, Quarto Series, vol. 18, 1911.) *Letters of Denization and Acts of Naturalization for Aliens in England and Ireland, 1701-1800*, (ed. William A. Shaw, publ. Huguenot Society of London, Quarto Series, vol. 27, 1923.) These list all aliens whatever their origin and are not confined to those of French or Huguenot descent.

Scotland: The records of naturalizations in Scotland before the Union in 1707 do not appear to be included in the indexes. If you are interested in a person who may have been naturalized in Scotland before 1707, the records should be in the Scottish Record Office in:

- letters of naturalization in the Register of the Privy Seal (mainly for the late 16th century);
- petitions recorded in the Register of the Privy Council; or
- letters patent under the Great Seal.

I know of no indexes to these naturalizations so you just have to take pot luck!

On the open shelves at Kew you should still be able to find the volumes of indexes of "Naturalization and Denization" running from 1509 to 1936. The indexes are organized in alphabetical order in distinct periods and you should always be careful to check that you are looking in all the alphabetical sequences in the relevant volume. Be certain also to look for all possible spellings you can think of; foreign names are a particularly rich source of spelling variations. It might be that you were unable to find the naturalization of your ancestor because TNA's Discovery catalogue has indexed him or her under a spelling you had not thought of. Possibly you knew them only from their anglicised name and they were indexed under their original German name – or vice versa! I still find it helpful to look through a paper list where you can go backwards and forwards looking for possible variants you may not have thought of. The indexes to records of Denization are in the same volumes as those of Naturalization but only extend to 1873.

Naturalization before 1844 involved getting a Private Act of Parliament and, as you can imagine, was very expensive. If you find a reference in the indexes to an Act, you will find that they are not held by TNA but by the Parliamentary Archives in the House of Lords Record Office, House of Lords, London, SW1A 0PW, where they can be seen and/or copied. The relevant Home Office correspondence, however, where it survives, is in TNA. Before 1844, or where a Private Act of Parliament is involved, there is not always a lot of personal information; though it is always worth looking for it. The Act normally only gives the parentage and place of origin, often a city rather than a State, of the person being naturalized.

Because of the expense involved in getting a Private Act and, no doubt, the parliamentary time they used up, an Act was passed enabling the Home Secretary to grant naturalization certificates without the need for a Private Act. This system came into use in 1844 and was the only system used after 1900.

During the period *1844 to 1900*, a naturalization is more likely to be under this administrative procedure than by Private Act. After 1844, the Home Office case file normally contains the applicant's "Memorial" giving his personal details: place of birth, age or actual birth date, parents' names (often including the mother's maiden name) and the parents' nationality. The papers also give the address(es) where the applicant has been living for the previous five years or more, his occupation and, sometimes, the name of the firm for which he has been working. If he was married to a foreign wife, her name and details, the date and place of marriage and the names and ages of the children under 21 years old and the addresses where they are living (if different from the father's address) are often given. This is because they too were covered by his naturalization. There should also be affidavits by five or more people who were British Subjects by birth saying how long they had known him and that he was a fit and proper person to be given British Nationality. There will also be the report by the police (after the First World War, MI5) saying he was a good citizen. As a general rule, the later the naturalization, the more information you can hope to find.

Ireland, Scotland and Wales: It is worth noting that these Home Office records include all denizations and naturalizations in the whole of the United Kingdom (ie England, Ireland, Scotland and Wales) from 1801 to 1980. After 1922, the Republic of Ireland had its own records which are in the Public Record Office in Dublin but the post 1922 records for Northern Ireland are with the other UK records at Kew.

The use of Private Acts to secure naturalization stopped in 1900.

For those aliens who were naturalized in UK after 1934, the Home Office copy of the naturalization certificate is seen as the main record and these mainly survive and are indexed in Discovery. However certificates for the period from June 1969 to June 1980 do not survive and Discovery only includes details from an index.

For naturalization certificates issued between 1981 and 1986 TNA's website provides a link to an online form you can use to request details of a naturalization certificate. For the period from 1st October 1986 you must apply to the UK Border Agency.

Records are normally closed to the public for 100 years but if you are interested in a naturalization which you are told is closed to the public, you should make an application under the Freedom of Information Act to be allowed access to the file. This can normally be done on TNA's website.

The surviving 1934-1968 Home Office case files are gradually being transferred from the Home Office to TNA in the series HO 405. Only about 40% of the files in that series survive. At the time of writing (May 2013) files for people with surnames beginning with the letters A to Q have been transferred and are in the Discovery catalogue; those for R to Z have not yet been transferred and to see them you should write to the Departmental Record Officer, Information and Record Management Service, 4th Floor, Seacole Building, Home Office, 2 Marsham Street, London, SW1P 4DF. Again, if you are told it is closed to the public, you should make an application under the Freedom of Information Act to be allowed access to the file.

Records of Aliens

In theory there was some control of aliens in the UK from the late 18th century but very few records relating to individuals survive. One early document is the Plymouth Aliens List covering Jewish aliens living in Plymouth in Devon in 1798 and updated in 1803 (*The Plymouth Aliens List 1798 and 1803* by V D Lipman in *Miscellanies Part VI*, The Jewish Historical Society of England, 1962, pp 187-194.) Most of the 58 aliens listed were from places that were later in Germany. The list survived in the records of the Jewish Congregation in Plymouth and it could be that there are other similar lists in other archives in the UK. Please let me know if you find any.

A Central Registry of Aliens was set up in 1914 but the Central Register itself no longer survives. Each local police force kept details of all registered aliens in their area. Those aliens who were not interned were required to report weekly to their local police station. Unfortunately virtually all the records once kept locally have been destroyed, usually by the relevant police force which had nowhere to keep the records! Some surviving aliens' registration cards for the (London) Metropolitan Police area have survived and are available at TNA in Class MEPO35. They relate to only about 1,000 aliens and cover 1884-1989 (ie the date of arrival in UK) but with a large proportion from around the 1930s. They will be in the Discovery catalogue. It is usually advisable to check in the local Police Museum or County Record Office covering the area where "your" alien lived to see if any records have survived.

From 1934 the Home Office kept a single series of Aliens' Personal Files covering all aliens coming to the UK for more than 3 months – not just those who naturalized. These files ceased when the individual died, finally left the Country or was naturalized. Where there was a pre-1934 file for the individual this was attached to and kept with the new file. These files were supposed to have been destroyed routinely after ceasing to be administratively relevant – ie when the alien died – but some have survived and are still in the Home Office and will be transferred to TNA in series H0405 in due course.

German Churches in the UK

The most comprehensive listing of information on these churches and their records is *The Records of German Churches of the British Isles 1550-1900, and other related records*, Research Guide Twelve, edited by Pam Freeman and published by the Anglo-German FHS, 2000.

If you have drawn a blank with the census and the naturalization records, another source that could give you the place of origin of your immigrant ancestor is the records of the German churches in the United Kingdom. The registers of all the churches listed below, with the exception of Christchurch (Christuskirche), Kensington, the Chapel Royal at St James's Palace, St Mark's, Fulham, and the Rev Schultze's registers from

Dublin, up to about 1914 have been indexed in the Anglo-German FHS Names Index (qv).

London

So many German-speakers moved to live and work in London that, from the 17th century, there have been Protestant churches in London holding services in German. Most of the Germans coming to London were Protestants because the neighbouring parts of Germany from which most immigrants came were mainly Protestant and also because, for much of the time, Catholics would have got a better reception in other Countries.

It was not uncommon for Germans in South East England to travel relatively long distances to attend services in their own churches and in their own language. These churches sometimes kept records of where their church members had come from in Germany and this is often noted in their records – the "Kirchenbücher", "Church Books" or parish registers, or even in the Pastors' notebooks kept with the individual church's general records. Two of the Anglo-German FHS's most indefatigable workers, Len Metzner and the late Pam Freeman, spent many years working through the records of all the German churches in England indexing the registers and locating, identifying and listing the other records.

The main German Protestant churches are the Lutheran and the Reformed or Calvinist Churches. Both are represented among the churches in London. The earliest were the Lutheran churches. The "Hamburger-Lutherische Kirche" or "Hamburg Lutheran Church" opened its doors in Little Trinity Lane in the City in 1669. It moved to Dalston in Hackney, next to the German Hospital, in the 1870s and the records are at the Guildhall Library. A history in German and English, *Hamburger Lutherische Kirche, London 1669-1969* was published in Germany in 1969.

Another contemporary Lutheran church was St Marienkirche or "St Mary in the Savoy" which was in the Liberty of the Savoy just off the Strand. Its name has now been transferred to the chapel in the basement of the International Lutheran Students' Centre in Sandwich Street, St Pancras. There are copy registers, in TNA in Class RG3, for 1669 to 1840. The church published a history in German and English, *St Mary's German Lutheran Church, London, 1694-1994* in 1994.

The next Lutheran church was St George's Lutheran Church in Little

St George's German Lutheran Church, Alie Street.

Alie Street, Aldgate, which was opened in 1763 and still exists – pictured left. It was specifically intended to serve the growing community of German sugar bakers in the East End. Sadly, declining congregations caused its closure as a church in November 1996 but the building has been taken over and restored by the Historic Chapels Trust. It is used for organ recitals, talks and the occasional service in German. If you want to see what an 18th or 19th century German Lutheran church looked like, you should arrange a visit. The box pews and the memorial tablets in German and English survive. The congregation has, however, been merged with that of St Marienkirche in St Pancras and the pre-20th century records of both churches have been deposited in Tower Hamlets Library. The Anglo-German FHS has indexed the registers of St George's from 1763 to 1895 though the registers do extend to the present day.

We have been less lucky with the German Reformed Church records. A German Reformed church, St Paul's, opened in the Savoy, off the Strand, in 1697. It moved several times: to an old Huguenot chapel in Dutchy Street, in 1771; when that was demolished in 1816 to make way for the approach to Waterloo Bridge, it moved to Hooper Square, Aldgate, from 1816 to 1887; and, when that building was purchased for a railway goods yard, to a purpose-built church in Goulston Street, Whitechapel, from 1887 until it was, ironically, bombed in the Second World War. The church was not replaced and the post War congregation shared St George's, Alie Street, with the Lutheran congregation. The moves have not been kind to the records and all that survives dates from 1824 – the records of the previous 127 years were deliberately destroyed by a discontented member of the parish council in 1824! The surviving records are at Tower Hamlets

Library with St George's. A history of 300 years of the German Reformed church in London was planned for 1997 but has not appeared; the best history is an article in the Anglo-German FHS magazine *Mitteilungsblatt*, no. 42, Sept. 1997, pp 15-17: *"300 Years of the German Reformed Church in London"* by Rudolf Muhs.

A German Roman Catholic Church, dedicated to St Boniface, the English monk from Devon who converted the heathen Germans, was opened in Whitechapel in 1862. It replaced a Chapel that had existed in the City from 1809. The records from 1812 are still at the church; rebuilt in modern style after being bombed in the Second World War. Most of the German Catholics in London at the time appear to have come from the nearer Roman Catholic parts of Germany: the Rhineland, the Palatinate (Pfalz), Baden and Württemberg with only a few from Bavaria proper and Austria. But be careful, one of the Anglo-German FHS members has found that, even after St Boniface's church was founded, her German Roman Catholic ancestors had at least one of their children baptised at St George's Lutheran Church. The churches are less than a mile apart so it can hardly have been a question of not being able to get to St Boniface. So if you cannot find an entry in the records of St Boniface, try St George's.

Before these special churches were built, and even afterwards when it suited them, German-speakers worshipped in the local Church of England parish churches or in other suitable churches. Lutheran worship was probably close enough to that of the Church of England for it not to worry either party. Many Reformed church members probably went to one of the many English non-conformist churches around and the Catholics went, like other Catholics, to where they could find a Catholic priest: you should look for their records among the other English Roman Catholic records of the period.

The earlier German churches were set up by the merchants and other middle class Germans but were open to all classes. However, the aristocracy tended to live in the West End and you will find many of them attending the churches in the Court suburbs of Kensington, Kew, etc. You will also find them in the German Lutheran Chapel Royal in the Palace of St James, founded in 1700 by Queen Anne, whose husband Prince George of Denmark was a Lutheran. *Memorials of St James's Palace* by Edgar Shepherd, London, Longmans, Green and Co., 1894, 2 vols. Vol II, pp 245-260, contains the most detailed history of the German Lutheran

Royal Chapel to date. The registers from 1712 to 1836 are among the non-conformist registers in TNA (in Class RG4/4568 & 4569) and can be searched online at **www.bmdregisters.co.uk**. I understand that those from 1866 onwards are in another German church: Christuskirche, Montpelier Place, Kensington, London SW7 1HL. Unfortunately the Anglo-German FHS has not been able to get access to that German church (which also has records of its own dating from 1904) and the registers are not indexed. Christuskirche also, apparently, holds the registers of St Marks, Fulham, from 1913 which also have not been indexed.

The public was also often allowed to use the various Embassy chapels from at least the 17th century onwards. That there are registers existing for various Catholic Chapels, like the Bavarian and Sardinian Embassy Chapels, is well known, but there were also Lutheran and Reformed Church Chapels. For example the Prussian Embassy Chapel in the 17th century had a Lutheran chaplain and it is probable that other German Embassies or Legations, besides the Swedish and Danish Embassies, had Lutheran or Calvinist chaplains. I have no idea where any of these chapels' registers, if any survive, may be and would welcome any information.

The German middle classes up to the end of the 18th century tended to live in and around the City and they were catered for by the Hamburg Lutheran Church and St Mary in the Savoy. The German working classes, especially the sugar bakers that started settling in London in the mid to late 18th century, tended to live and work in Whitechapel and Stepney. The church of St George in Alie Street was specifically built for the sugar bakers of Whitechapel and Aldgate and, over the next 150 years, the large working class German community in East London used it. Many, however, especially those that married English girls, used the Church of England parish churches: the registers of St Mary, Whitechapel, and St George in the East are full of German names. My own Weyman family, Johann Friedrich having married an English girl in St Mary, Whitechapel, had all the children baptised in one or other of those two churches. However, as he got older, his thoughts must have returned to his German roots for his burial in 1847 appears in the register of the German Reformed church: St Paul, Hooper Square. Perhaps he attended the German services there while his wife and children attended the Church of England? Unfortunately his is one of the very few entries that does not give the deceased's place of origin in Germany. Possibly no-one at the Church knew where he had come from.

As the 19th century progressed, the German community in London increased considerably, those who had done well in business moved out to the new suburbs and new, well-off, middle class refugees arrived. This led to the founding of new German churches in the suburbs: the Camberwell Evangelical Church in 1854; the Islington Lutheran Church in 1856 and the Sydenham Evangelical Church (now called the Dietrich Bonhoeffer Evangelical Church) in 1875. The registers of those churches up to about 1914 have been indexed and are on the Anglo-German FHS Name Index.

England and Wales outside London

In most cases there were no German churches and you must look for Germans' baptisms, marriages and burials in the usual places. For example there was a large influx of German miners from Augsburg into Cornwall, South Wales and Cumbria in the 16th century. The Germans appear in the local registers from then on; especially in Keswick and Coniston where a relatively large German group settled and was gradually absorbed into the local community over the centuries. *Germans at Coniston in the Seventeenth Century*, by W G Collingwood, MA, FSA, in *Transactions of the Cumberland & Westmorland Antiquarian & Archaeological Society*, Vol X, New Series, pp 369-394.1910, contains detailed lists of the Germans that appear in the parish registers of Crosthwaite and Coniston. See also: *Elizabethan Keswick. Extracts from the Original Account Books, 1564-1577, of the German Miners in the Archives of Augsburg*, by W G Collingwood, publ. 1912; reprinted, 1987, by Michael Moon's Bookshop, 41, 42 & 43 Roper Street, Whitehaven, Cumbria.

Similarly a large group of swordmakers from Solingen came to Shotley Bridge in County Durham in the 1680s to make sword blades for the British Army and their names appear in the local registers for generations after. For their story see *The Shotley Bridge Swordmakers – Their Strange History* by David Richardson, Northern History Booklet No. 37. Publ. Frank Graham, 6 Queen's Terrace, Newcastle upon Tyne, NE2 2PL, 1973,

It was not until the mid 19th century that German Protestant churches (I do not know of any German Catholic churches outside London) started appearing outside London. Those that I am aware of in England are: Liverpool, founded 1846; Hull, Yorkshire, founded 1848; Manchester, founded 1855; Brighton, Sussex, founded 1862 (though with no known registers); Sunderland, County Durham, founded 1863; Bradford, Yorkshire, founded 1876; South Shields, County Durham, founded 1879; and Newcastle upon Tyne, founded 1906. It is clear from the locations that many were intended to serve the German merchant seamen and the craftsmen, tradesmen and merchants who settled in the sea ports or where the cotton and woollen industries were booming. In many cases, besides the church registers, other records have survived and there are even some published histories, eg *The Hull German Lutheran Church 1848-1998* by Barbara M. Robinson, published in English by Highgate Publications (Beverley) Ltd, 4 Newbegin, Beverley, HU17 8EG; *Hundert Jahre Evangelische Gemeinde Deutscher Sprache, German Speaking Lutheran Congregation, Newcastle upon Tyne, 1881-1981*, published by the church in German in about 1981; and *Geschichte der Deutschen Evangelischen Kirche in Liverpool* by D. Lic. Albert Eduard Rosenkranz, published in German in Düsseldorf in 1965.

Scotland
I am only aware of one German church in Scotland: the German Protestant church in Edinburgh. The records are in the Scottish Record Office and baptism and burial registers survive from 1884 and confirmation and marriage registers from 1885. The Church was there much earlier, from 1862, and there is also a list of members from 1864 to 1885, and other records surviving from the 1870s. There are known to have been German communities in Glasgow, and other Scottish cities, especially where there were sugar refineries, or major seaports. However I know of no churches or permanent congregations.

Ireland
A German Lutheran church was founded in Marlborough Street in Dublin in 1697 moving to a purpose built church in Poolbeg Street in 1725 where it remained for the next 100 years. The community appears to have disappeared by 1850, when the church burned down, and it was not until 1930 that German services were held again in Dublin. There is a history in German and English, *The Lutheran Church in Ireland, 1697-1997*,

published by Monika McCurdy & Alan Murphy for the Evangelisch-Lutherische Kirche in Irland, Lutherhaus, 24 Adelaide Road, Dublin, 1997. Sadly I have no knowledge of what happened to the records of this church other than two baptism and marriage registers of the Rev Schultze covering 1806-37 which are held by the Registrar-General for Ireland in Dublin (and contain many irregular marriages). I know of no other German churches in Ireland. It is likely that wherever Germans settled in Ireland they used the local parish churches and it is there that you should look for their baptisms, marriages and burials, if those registers survive. Even where there were large settlements, as with the Palatines of 1710 who settled on Sir Thomas Southwell's estate at Rathkeale, County Limerick, and on the estate of Abel Ram at Gorey, County Wexford, the settlers used the local Church of Ireland parish churches – at least until Methodism provided an alternative.

Church Schools

The Germans seem to have put more weight on providing a good education for their children than most contemporary English people. The churches were the main providers of education and as early as 1708 in London there was a German school attached to the German church of St Mary in the Savoy. There was also a "poor house" nearby. The records of those bodies do not appear to survive in any amounts. The Church published an illustrated booklet, in German, in 1908 to commemorate the 200th anniversary of the school and one of the Society's members, Amanda Price, has translated it into English as: *200 Years of the German School in London, 1708-1908*. Sadly the school did not survive the First World War. Records do however survive for the St George's German Lutheran Church, Alie Street, boys' and girls' Infants School. The school buildings adjoined the church in Alie Street and were converted into flats in 1998-99. The records listing pupils from 1828 to 1917 (when the school was closed by the British Government) have been indexed by Len Metzner and are available for searches in the Anglo-German FHS Names Index.

Charities

The records of the "Ladies' Clothing Society" of St George's German Lutheran Church, Alie Street, out-relief for members of the German community who had fallen on hard times, survive for 1821-1846 and

1863-1868. Those records and those of applicants for pensions from the Society of Friends of Foreigners in Distress, were indexed by Christiane Swinbank when she was preparing her thesis on Germans in 19th century London. They are not in the Society's Name Index but can be accessed through the Anglo-German FHS.

I was lucky enough to find the family of my own German immigrant in the Ladies' Clothing Society records and gained an insight into how difficult their lives were in the 1820s when the main breadwinner was sick and returned, alone, to Germany to recover, leaving his wife and young children to fend for themselves. The entry reads:

May 1827: Frederick Wayman has been a laborer in a Sugarhouse, but has been obliged to go to Germany about a twelve month ago, on account of the miserable state of his health; since when his wife, a very decent nice woman, has endeavored to support herself & her children by washing; her family consists of 3 Boys, the two eldest of whom go to School at 2d a week; the boys are aged 7 years 6 months; 5 years & 2 years 6 months.

Jan 1830: Having returned from Germany in better health he is now employed again in a Sugarhouse at £20 yearly wages & 10s a week for Board wages. This family not being therefore in great distress it was resolved to give etc. boy aged 10 (who attends our School) usual articles, boy aged 8, boy aged 5, boy aged 1.

Possibly Frederick had bronchitis or some such illness caused by London's polluted air and needed to recover in the country air of his German home. He did not die until March 1847, aged 61 and a scum boiler. The cause of death was inflammation of the lungs so he might well have suffered, as many would have done, from air pollution. His wife, Susan, was English-born but the German community still helped even though the family does not appear to have attended any of the German churches. The connection might have been recognized by the Ladies because the eldest sons attended the St George Alie Street School. My ancestor, Wernint Wayman, was the 5 year old in 1827.

The German Orphanage
There was also a German Orphanage, "Deutsches Waisenhaus" 106 Norfolk Road, at Dalston in Hackney, London from 1879 to 1939 and a girls' home called "Lutherhaus", opposite the German Church in Dalston, from 1932 to 1939. Unfortunately there are no known surviving records except for plans of the orphanage among the German Hospital (qv) records.

Jewish Records
Many immigrants, particularly in the mid to late 19th century and in the 20th century were Jewish. They should appear in the same civil sources as gentile immigrants but, in place of the church records, they should of course, be sought in the records of the synagogues.

Jewish immigrants were more likely than Christian immigrants to naturalize and there were several Jewish Charities that encouraged them to do so. So your first port of call should be the naturalization records outlined above.

The Society of Genealogists publishes *My Ancestors were Jewish*, by Dr Anthony Joseph, 2008, which is a very helpful introduction to Jewish research in UK. Also, the Jewish Genealogical Society of Great Britain (JGSGB) is producing a very useful series of booklets including *Jewish Ancestors? A Guide to Jewish Genealogy in the United Kingdom*, edited by Rosemary Wenzerul, JGSGB, 2011, and *Jewish Ancestors? A Guide to Jewish Genealogy in Germany and Austria*, edited by Thea Skyte, Randol Schoenberg & Rosemary Wenzerul, JGSGB, 2001. Other JGSGB guides relate to researching Jewish Ancestors from Lithuania (revised 2011) by Sam Aaron; from Poland by Sue Fifer; and from Latvia and Estonia by Arlene Beare. There are also other useful JGSGB publications on *Genealogical Resources within the Jewish Home and Family* and *A Guide to Reading Hebrew Inscriptions and Documents* both by Rosemary Wenzerul.

Particularly useful if you have Jewish ancestors in UK in the mid-19th century are *The Jewish Victorian. Genealogical Information from the Jewish Newspapers 1861-1870* transcribed and edited by Doreen Berger, published 2004 and the sister volume covering 1871-1880, also by Doreen Berger, published in 1999. The amount of genealogical information in these volumes is incredible!

An older but still useful publication is the more detailed section on Jewish research by Edgar R. Samuel in *Sources for Roman Catholic and Jewish Genealogy and Family History*, by Don Steel, National Index of Parish Registers Volume 3, published by Phillimore & Co, Chichester, 1974.

If you are interested in research into Jewish immigrants from Germany and elsewhere in Europe you really should join the JGSGB which publishes an excellent quarterly magazine *Shemot*, in English, and has a very useful website at **www.jgsgb.org.uk**. Their Special Interest Groups (SIGs) are a major source of expertise covering different geographical areas of Europe.

If you cannot find your German ancestor in UK in the period before civil registration, it is worth considering whether they may have been Jewish originally. Some Jews, like Benjamin Disraeli's father, were converted to Christianity and many married gentile wives or husbands.

Records of the British Armed Services

The Army
The records of the British Army, Royal Navy and Royal Marines are full of German names. The British Crown often hired regiments of German mercenary soldiers to serve in its armies during wartime. The Hessians and Waldeckers of the American War of Independence are some of the better known examples. In such cases the regiment was generally hired as a unit and the Treasury paid the money direct to the German Prince concerned; any surviving records of individuals, therefore, would be in Germany. Up to 1794, individual Germans and other foreigners could enlist in British regiments: for example it was quite fashionable in the 18th century for British regiments to have German drill sergeants. The law did not allow the setting up, as part of the British Army, of regiments composed wholly or mainly of foreigners. There were, however, some British Regiments, like the 60th Foot, to which individual German, Swiss, and other foreign-born recruits were usually posted. The law was changed in 1794 and allowed the raising of "auxiliary" regiments from foreign-born recruits. These included many Germans. In these cases the regiments were part of the British Army and the records are at TNA, Kew. For more details see *Foreign Regiments in the British Army 1793-1802* by

A soldier of the King's German Legion.

C. T. Atkinson, Journal of the Society for Army Historical Research, Vols. XXI-XXII (1942-1944); *The Auxiliaries: Foreign and Miscellaneous Regiments in the British Army 1802-1817* by R. L. Yaple, Journal of the Society for Army Historical Research, Vol. L (1972). These articles provide potted histories of all the Regiments concerned and provide pointers as to which had large German contingents.

The main component of German troops in the British Army during the Napoleonic Wars was the King's German Legion (KGL). The main history of the KGL is *History of the King's German Legion*, by N. Ludlow

Beamish, FRS, 2 vols, 1832-37, reprinted by Naval & Military Press, Dallington, East Sussex, 1997. The Anglo-German FHS publishes two much cheaper, but useful and well-illustrated books: *The King's German Legion: Records and Research* and *The King's German Legion: Records and Research 2*, both edited by Gwen Davis. There may soon be a third volume.

The KGL was formed when the Electorate of Hanover (of which King George III was the Elector) was conquered by Napoleon in 1803. The Royal Hanoverian army was disbanded but large numbers escaped to England where in August 1803 they were reformed into the KGL. They served in most of the theatres of war including the Peninsula and, most famously, at Waterloo where they distinguished themselves, especially in the defence of La Haye Sainte. They were disbanded as part of the British Army and returned to Hanover where they were recreated as the Royal Hanoverian Army in 1815. While in exile they were stationed in England: the main base being at Bexhill, Sussex, the cavalry at Ipswich, Suffolk, and the engineers at Weymouth, Dorset. The records are voluminous and have largely been indexed by Len Metzner for the Anglo-German FHS Names Index (qv).

The British Government was raising regiments of foreigners as late as the outbreak of the Crimean War in 1854. The British German Legion, made up mainly of Germans though some came from USA, was first based at Shorncliffe in Kent for training in early 1855. The first troops left for the Crimea in October 1855 but arrived too late to take part in the fighting.

Even after the armistice was signed in April 1856, German recruits continued to arrive in England. In July 1856 the British German Legion was marched to other barracks: some to Aldershot in Hampshire and some to Colchester in Essex to be disbanded and repatriated. Most went back to Germany or joined other Countries' Armies. The best current source for the history of these British Foreign Legions is *Mercenaries for the Crimea. The German, Swiss and Italian Legions in British Service. 1854-1856* by C F Bayley, published by McGill-Queen's University Press, Montreal, 1977.

After the Crimean War, the British Government in South Africa wanted to recruit some of the German Legionaries to the Cape Colony Police. These jobs were supposed to be for married men only so there was a flurry of marriages of German soldiers to English girls. For example, in Colchester Garrison Church there were 150 such marriages in October 1856 – 64 on one day: 20th October 1856. The records of the British German Legion are among the War Office records in TNA, Kew, and most have been indexed by Len Metzner and included in the Anglo-German FHS's Name Index (qv). Some of the Germans were also subsequently recruited from England and from Cape Colony to help to put down the Indian Mutiny and they appear among the records of the Indian Army in the British Library's India Office Library and Records, which are in the British Library at St Pancras.

So far as records of the British Army generally are concerned, TNA's "Discovery" catalogue indexes the service records of those soldiers who applied for pensions from Chelsea Hospital or the Irish equivalent, Kilmainham Hospital. These should cover most men who did not die while still serving and extend from about 1760 until 1913. There is also a very useful, free series of guides to Army records on the National Archives website under "Records". The best general books on researching British Army soldiers are *Army Records. A Guide for Family Historians* by William Spencer, TNA, 2008, and *My Ancestor was in the British Army*, by Michael & Christopher Watts, published by the Society of Genealogists, 2009.

Many German immigrants joined the local Militia, the then equivalent of the Territorial Army, and may be found in their records. The attestation (ie joining) records of the Militia 1806-1915 are available online on **www.findmypast.co.uk**. The best general guide to using Militia records is *Records of the Militia & Volunteer Forces 1757-1945* by William Spencer, PRO Reader's Guide No 3, 1997, but, again, there are useful free guides on TNA's website under "Records".

There is also a very useful census of men serving in the British Army in 1861 provided by Roger E Nixon. It is available on the subscription website, **www.findmypast.co.uk**. It provides the names, ranks, army numbers and regiments of about 98% of "other ranks" serving in the British Army at that time. A small number, estimated at about 5,000 men, are not included because the pay lists listing their names have not survived. It includes records not only of "other ranks" serving in Britain, but also of those serving in the Army overseas. For this reason, it can be an exceptionally useful source in identifying men missing from the 1861 census returns.

Most of the service records of British Army "other ranks" who served in the First World War were destroyed by bombing during the Second World War. Only about 40% survive. Again TNA's website under "Records" provides several useful, free guides to the surviving records. TNA's "Discovery" catalogue indexes the First World War Medal Index Cards, which are the most complete surviving listing. To see the actual card on screen you would have to pay but, if you already have a subscription to **www.ancestry.co.uk**, you can see and print the MIC for no extra fee. For virtually all British Army officers for the period, the personal files do survive and are indexed on "Discovery". The files themselves are not available to download online and you will need to pay to have them copied at Kew. The best general book on researching First World War Army ancestors is *Army Service Records of the First World War* by Simon Fowler, William Spencer & Stuart Tamblin, PRO Readers' Guide No 19, published in 1997.

Another very useful site, and free to search and download from, is that of the Commonwealth War Graves Commission (CWGC) which indexes all those in the services of the Commonwealth who were killed in wars in the 20th century, with details of their deaths and memorials. It also includes civilians.

Many of the people in these indexes could be Germans or of German descent.

The Royal Navy and Royal Marines

The Royal Marine and Royal Navy records contain details of large numbers of Germans at all periods before the early 20th century. There are no records that specifically deal with Germans but the records are generally good and many ships, particularly during the Napoleonic Wars, had a number of foreigners on board – sometimes Germans. There is no consolidated index except from the mid 19th century to WW1 and you have to look through the individual ship's Muster Book and Description Book where they survive. These give the man's age and place of birth; often giving the actual town or village. You therefore need the name of the ship. Royal Marine Description Books contain the same details. *Tracing your Naval Ancestors* by Bruno Pappalardo, TNA Readers' Guide No. 24, is the best book on the records of the Royal Navy. On the Royal Marines the best book is *My Ancestor was a Royal Marine*, by Ken Divall, published by the Society of Genealogists in 2008. But I still also use: *Records of the Royal Marines* by Garth Thomas, PRO Readers Guide No 10, HMSO, 1994.

TNA's "Discovery" catalogue indexes by name the service records of Royal Navy ratings who joined between 1853 and 1923, officers who joined between 1756 and 1931, Royal Marine marines who joined between 1842 and 1926 and Royal Marine officers who joined between 1793 and 1925. Once again you will find the free guides on aspects of Naval records on TNA's website, under "Records", useful.

British Campaign Medals
It is also possible to search the medal rolls covering campaign medals 1793 to 1949. Those records (in Class WO100) are searchable by name in **www.ancestry.co.uk**. A useful book on British medals is *Medals. A Researcher's Guide* by William Spencer, TNA, 2004. The best guide to British medals generally is the annual publication, *Medal Yearbook* published by Token Publishing, which lists and illustrates each British medal, and those awarded by Commonwealth Governments.

Most British and Commonwealth medals incorporate the name, rank, number and regiment, corps or ship, of the recipient (the most obvious exception being the British campaign medals for the Second World War). Men of German descent, so long as they were British Subjects, may have volunteered to join the services from 1914 in the First World War and were subject to conscription like everyone else from 1916 and during the Second World War. So they too could have received the same medals.

The Merchant Navy
Many Germans served as seamen, mates and masters in the British Merchant Marine. This was often, no doubt, because the British Merchant Marine, being considerably larger, offered sailors a wider choice of berths than the German equivalent. Again there are no special records that relate solely to Germans and you have to use the records of the Registrar General of Shipping and Seamen now at TNA, Kew. TNA's website, under "Records" has some useful free guides on the Merchant Navy. The best book on the Merchant Navy records is *My Ancestor was a Merchant*

Seaman, by Christopher and Michael Watts, published by the Society of Genealogists, 2004.

The records of Merchant Navy seamen really only start in 1835 but there are earlier records relating to apprenticeships from 1824. There is a gap in the records of seamen between 1857 and 1918 but those from 1918 are now available on microfilm at TNA, Kew. The original cards are held in the Southampton Archives but on **www.findmypast.co.uk** you can download copies of the cards which usually include an identity photograph of the seaman.

If you know the name of the ship your ancestor sailed on you can, with some detective work, consult the Crew Lists which give the ages and places of birth of each of the crew. The best starting place is the Crew List Index Project or CLIP. Go to **www.crewlist.co.uk** which should help you to find the crew lists for ships sailing in the period 1861 to 1913.

Separate records of Merchant Navy masters and mates run from 1845 and there are detailed records of their services in the Board of Trade records at TNA and in the Lloyds of London records at the London Metropolitan Archives. www.ancestry.co.uk now has a database of Masters' and Mates' certificates 1850-1927.

Against the general rule that only the wealthier immigrants are likely to have bothered with naturalization, it is worth checking in the case of merchant seamen as there were special rules allowing them to naturalize without paying. You also often get a list of all the British ships they had sailed on for the previous seven years or so.

Hon. East India Company

I have already mentioned that some of the men of the British German Legion were recruited to help put down the Indian Mutiny in 1857 and can be found among the records of the Indian Army. India was also a magnet to Germans at other periods: as soldiers, merchants, explorers, missionaries, seamen or even as civil servants. The records of the East India Company Army, Navy, Merchant Navy and Civil Service and the ordinary records of the births, marriages and deaths of Christians in the subcontinent, and the records of the India Office and the British Government of India 1861-1949 are available at the British Library in Euston Road, St Pancras, in Central London.

If you have German ancestry in British India (which includes the present states of India, Pakistan and Bangladesh) you should join the Families in British India Society (see **www.new.fibis.org**). They publish several useful leaflets on how to research in the archives of the sub-continent especially those in the British Library.

The City of London

One of the magnets that drew German immigrants to the UK was the City of London itself where they hoped to make their fortune (and many did!). Most people know of the Rothschild banking family, whose founder in England was Nathan Mayer von Rothschild who came to London from Frankfurt am Main and founded the bank, N M Rothschild & Sons, in 1811. Barings Bank was founded in 1762 by Francis Baring whose father, Johann Baring, was a clothier in Exeter but had been born in Bremen, the son of a Lutheran pastor. Andreas Grote (1710-86) also came from Bremen and founded a banking partnership in 1766 which later was absorbed in the Royal Bank of Scotland.

To set up in business in the City of London, even just to open a shop, you had to be a British Subject and so any alien had to naturalize first. They also had to be a member of one of the London Livery Companies. If they had not served an apprenticeship, they would have had to purchase membership and the Livery Company's records would record that. When they became Freemen of the City, the Corporation of London's record of the fact would say which Livery Company they were a member of but also when they became naturalized.

The records of the Corporation of London, which include the Freedom records, are now held in London Metropolitan Archives and you can download a free leaflet, *City Freedom Archives* from their website. The records of Freedoms are comprehensive after 1681 (there are some earlier records but they are fragmentary) and the most useful source is the City Freedom Admission papers 1681-1925 which are available to read and download on **www.ancestry.co.uk**. *My Ancestor was a Freeman of the City of London*, by Vivienne E. Aldous, published by the Society of Genealogists in 1999, is a good introduction.

The "Poor Palatines" encamped on Blackheath, 1709.

Immigration Records

The Palatines of 1709
The largest early influx of Germans to England was that of the "Poor Palatines" in 1709. The British Government of the time wanted to encourage the settlement of Protestants in New England to act as a buffer against the threat of the Catholic French in Quebec. They decided to encourage poor Protestant Germans from the Palatinate (the Pfalz), to come to England before being shipped to New York. The response was much larger than they had expected and poor Germans arrived at Rotterdam in their thousands. Most of the Treasury lists of the Germans being shipped from Rotterdam, and those landed in London over the summer of 1709, survive.

There were 30,000 Germans, men, women and children, camped on Blackheath over much of the winter of 1709. The British Government changed while this was going on and the new Government had less interest in the scheme but the Germans were there and needed to be looked after. In the end some were shipped to New England, some settled in Ireland, over half (including all the Catholics!) appear to have been sent back to Germany, and some probably stayed in London and merged into the local population. I have not actually discovered anyone with a proven descent from a Palatine who stayed in England and would be very interested to hear from anyone who has.

As most of the Palatines went on to New England or Ireland, the best books available are, not surprisingly, by an American: Hank Z. Jones. They are *The Palatine Families of Ireland*, by Henry Z. Jones Jr, 2nd ed, Picton Press, Camden, Maine, 1990; *The Palatine Families of New York, 1710* by Henry Z. Jones Jr, 2 vols, published by Henry Z. Jones Jr,

Universal City, California, 1985; *More Palatine Families* by Henry Z. Jones Jr, published by Henry Z. Jones Jr, Universal City, California, 1991. All these books are effectively biographical dictionaries of the families descended from the original immigrants with details of their origins in Germany. If you are interested in the Irish Palatines (and if you can find a copy!), I can recommend *People Make Places. The Story of the Irish Palatines*, by Patrick J. O'Connor, published by Oireacht na Mumhan Books, Newcastle West, Co Limerick, in 1989. This is a detailed history of the Palatine migration with particular emphasis on the families that settled in Ireland. Amongst the typical Anglicised (or should that be Hibernicised!) surnames are Bovenizer, Dolmage and Embury.

Ships' Passenger Lists and Aliens' Certificates

In most cases passengers arriving in England from German or other European ports were not recorded, or the records were not kept, until about the mid 19th century. However, in TNA at Kew in the Home Office records are Ships' Lists of Aliens (HO3/1-102) which cover the period 1836 to 1860 & 1867 to 1869 and give the alien's name, trade and, in some cases, place of birth/origin. These lists were deposited by the ship's master on the ship's arrival in a UK port. There is a partial index to these records from 1847 to 1852, again by Len Metzner, which can be searched in the TNA or through the Anglo-German FHS Names Index; the index covers all those entries that gave a German place as the origin of the individual but some of the entries were illegible and, obviously, are not included.

Aliens' Certificates for the period 1836 to 1852 which are in HO2 are kept under the port of arrival in Great Britain. They give the alien's nationality, profession, date of arrival, last country visited and his signature. There is an index in HO5/25-32 which covers the Aliens' Certificates issued between 1826 and 1849. The certificates from 1826 to 1835 have not survived but the index itself can be helpful in indicating when and where an immigrant arrived here. Len Metzner has indexed HO2/213-228 covering all of 1852 and the returns for London and Folkestone for 1851, subject to the same caveats as HO3 above, so the only year missing from an index is 1850 and the returns from Dover for 1851. Len Metzner's indexes are in the Anglo-German FHS Names Index (qv).

The subscription website, **www.ancestry.co.uk**, now includes scanned copies of all the surviving ships' passenger lists and aliens' certificates and has provided its own index. A word of warning though: many of these documents are in the old German script and not very legible so the indexing is not always very reliable. It would pay you to check the indexes produced by Len Metzner in case he has identified your ancestor but ancestry.co.uk has missed him!

One particularly helpful set of records in **www.ancestry.co.uk**, that Len Metzner did not cover, is the list of Alien arrivals between August 1810 and May 1811 (FO 83/21-22). They are handwritten by English clerks so the indexing should not be a problem.

German Occupations

German immigrants were, of course, as likely as the next immigrant to turn their hands to whatever work was available. However, you should not expect to find a German immigrant as eg a farm labourer in the English midland shires, unless he was a POW in WW2 and stayed on. At particular times, German immigrants were heavily represented in particular occupations. I have already mentioned the miners that came over to Cornwall, South Wales and Cumberland in the 16th century and the armed services in the Napoleonic period.

During the period from the accession of George I in 1714 to the death of William IV in 1837, the King of Great Britain was also the Elector of Hanover and had to rule both countries. While he was resident in London, the Government of Hanover had offices and quite a large civil service in Westminster and many Hanoverians consequently lived and died here. The court also brought with it many German tradesmen who provided the courtiers with the goods, music, food, etc they were accustomed to in Hanover – ie tailors, composers, artists, wig makers, grocers, etc. Many of them, and their children, settled here.

Less obvious was the effective monopoly Germans had on the **sugar industry**, especially in London, from the mid 18th century to the mid 19th century. By the mid 19th century Stepney and Whitechapel in London were heavily populated by German-born sugar bakers; in the 1851 census you find whole streets where the adults were all born in Germany and the males are "sugar bakers" or "scum boilers" or some such term. These were the labourers who were willing to work long hours in dangerous and debilitating circumstances for relatively low pay. Contrary to some family traditions sugar bakers were not confectioners (though many of those were Germans too) but people who worked in factories refining sugar from the raw sugar cane that came in through the docks.

Sugarbakers. From Sweat to Sweetness by Bryan Mawer, published by the Anglo-German FHS, 2011, gives a comprehensive history and description of the trade. Bryan Mawer also has a very comprehensive website listing thousands of sugar refiners, mainly German or of German ancestry, see **www.mawer.clara.net**.

In the period of the Napoleonic Wars, when my own ancestor Johan Friedrich Weyman came to London as a sugarbaker, it appears that sugarbakers are likely to have come from Bremen, Hamburg and north western Hannover – the Duchy of Bremen-Verden. The map on page 40 shows that area, known as the Elbe-Weser-Dreieck (Triangle), showing the places of origin of many sugarbaker emigrants to the UK.

The sugar refineries, because of the nature of the refining process, were very liable to catch fire, and so the sugar refiners found it very difficult to get fair rates of fire insurance. Being mainly Germans, they also felt that they were subject to some anti-alien prejudice. They therefore set up their own insurance company in 1782 to insure themselves. That insurance company became the Phoenix Insurance Company and the Company's archives are held at Cambridge University Library. See **www.mawer.clara.net** under "Phoenix Fire Office" for details..

The German Hospital at Dalston in Hackney was founded 'for the reception of all poor Germans and others speaking the German language'. It also cared for the local English-speaking population in the case of emergencies. It was supported by subscriptions and donations, many from Germany or the German community in England, and was run by German nursing sisters and doctors. Nursing care was provided by the Protestant Deaconesses from the Kaiserswerth Institute near Wessendorf. It was their example at "the German" which prompted Florence Nightingale to visit the Hospital on two occasions and then to enrol for training at the Institute in Germany in 1851.

During the First World War, the German staff remained at the Hospital despite strong anti-German feelings in the country and a shortage of nurses and doctors in Germany. The hospital, however, was closed by the British Government during the Second World War and taken over by the NHS

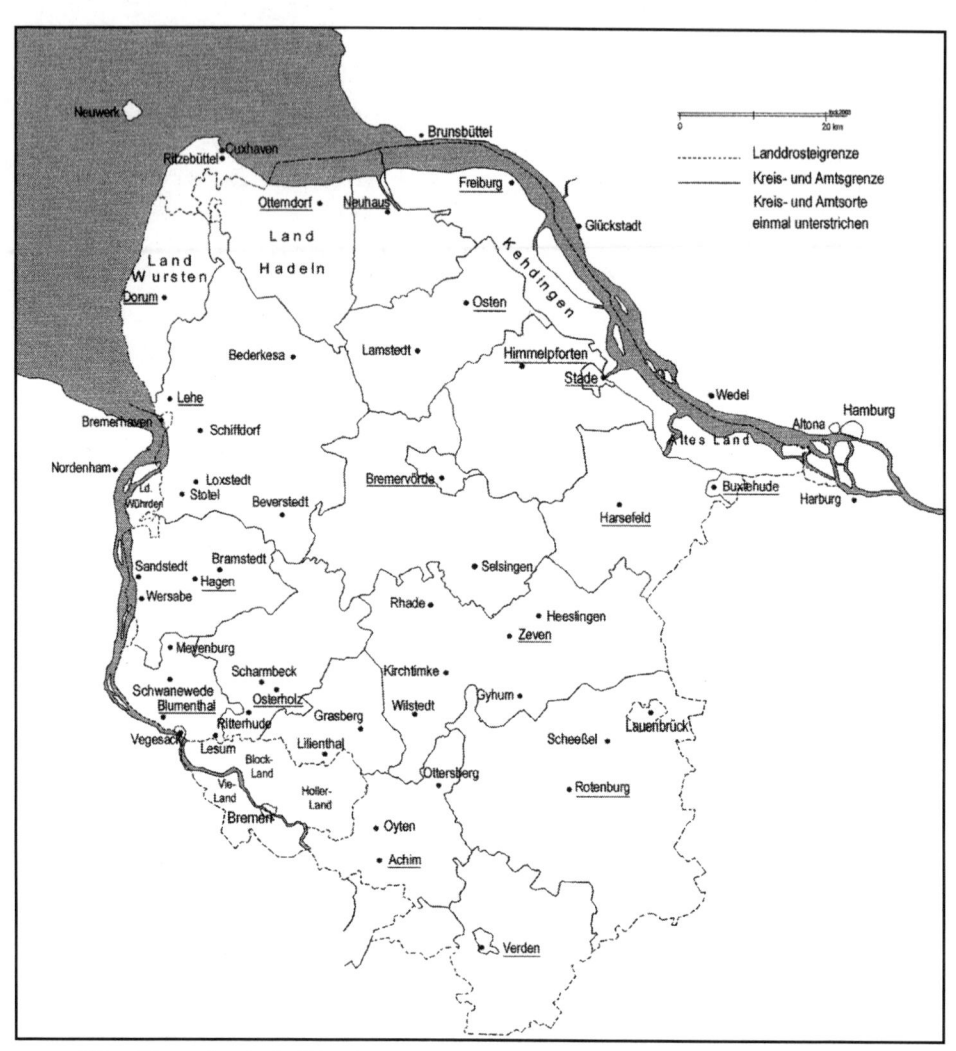

Elbe-Weser-Dreieck, District (Landdrostei) of Stade, Kingdom of Hanover, with bailiwicks (Amtsbezirke), seats of bailiffs (Amtssitze) and places of origin of migrants to UK. (map by Thomas Fock based on an original by Henry Lange, 1859)

The German Hospital at Dalston.

after the War. The buildings still survive though they are no longer used by the NHS and have mainly been converted into flats. *The German Hospital in London and the Community it served 1845 to 1948* by Maureen Specht, published by the Anglo-German FHS, 1997, provides a detailed history of the hospital and the German doctors and nurses who worked there. The Hospital's administrative records survive in large quantities and are kept at the Royal Hospitals NHS Trust Archives at St Bartholomew's Hospital, West Smithfield, London, EC1A 7BE. We have recently discovered that some patients' records 1898-1926 are held in the Wellcome Library at 183 Euston Road, London, NW1 2BE; website: **library@wellcome.ac.uk**.

Large numbers of Germans also came as:
- **bakers** – by the beginning of the First World War, a large proportion of the bakers in London had German names and questions were asked about it in Parliament.
- **pork butchers** – Sue Gibbons has researched and edited a book, *German Pork Butchers in Britain*, published for the Anglo-German FHS in 2001. Most came from the Kingdom of Württemberg, now in southwest Germany and, indeed, new research in Germany seems to

GERMAN HOSPITAL
DALSTON.

UNDER THE PROTECTION OF

HIS MOST GRACIOUS MAJESTY THE KING

HIS MAJESTY THE GERMAN EMPEROR, KING OF PRUSSIA;
HIS APOSTOLIC MAJESTY THE EMPEROR OF AUSTRIA, KING OF HUNGARY;
His Royal Highness The Prince of Wales.
And under the PATRONAGE of most of the EUROPEAN SOVEREIGNS.

President - HIS ROYAL HIGHNESS THE DUKE OF CONNAUGHT.

THE SIXTY-FIFTH ANNIVERSARY
DINNER
Of the Patrons and Friends of the above Institution will take place

ON THURSDAY, MAY 19TH, 1910,
AT THE
"WHITEHALL ROOMS,"
HOTEL METROPOLE
(Entrance from Whitehall Place.)

The Right Hon.
SIR FRANK CAVENDISH LASCELLES
IN THE CHAIR. G.C.B., G.C.M.G., C.V.O.

DINNER ON TABLE AT HALF-PAST SIX, FOR SEVEN O'CLOCK, P.M., PRECISELY.

VICE-PRESIDENTS AND HONORARY STEWARDS.

His Excellency COUNT METTERNICH.
His Excellency COUNT MENSDORFF.
His Excellency COUNT BENCKENDORFF.
His Excellency BARON GERICKE VAN HERWIJNEN.
His Excellency MONSIEUR GASTON OARLIN.
His Excellency COUNT DE LALAING.
His Excellency COUNT WRANGEL.
Dr. H. JOHANNES, Privy Councillor of Legation and Consul-General of the German Hospital.
BARON ALFRED DE ROTHSCHILD, I. & R. Austro-Hungarian Hon. Consul-General.

BARON HEYKING, D.C.L., Ph.D., Consul-General of Russia.
EDWARD POLLET, Esq., Consul-General of Belgium.
DANIEL DANIELSSON, Esq., Consul-General of Sweden.
H. S. J. MAAS, Esq., K.N.L., Council-General of the Netherlands.
BARON BRUNO VON SCHRÖDER (Treasurer).
BARON ERLANGER.
E. BORGMANN, Esq.
MAX G. FLEMMING, Esq.
PAUL VOIGT, Esq.
ERNEST L. WALFORD, Esq.

TICKETS (21s. each) may be had of the Stewards; of Mr. W. F. Cochrane, the Secretary, at the Hospital; or at the Hotel Metropole.

The Musical Arrangements will be under the eminent direction of CHEVALIER WILHELM GANZ.

Advertising a fund-raising dinner for the German Hospital.

show that many of them came from the even more localised region of Hohenlohe.
- **ladies' and gentlemen's hairdressers** – *German Hairdressers in the UK. Their effect upon the British Way of Life*, by Jenny Towey, published by the Anglo-German FHS in 2004, provides a detailed history of the trade and lists a good number of the German hairdressers in UK. In the 19th century, at least in London, Germans appear to have taken the role in the trade that the French and Italians took in the 20th century.
- **merchant seamen** – see section on "The Merchant Navy" (pages 33–34) above.
- **artists** – eg Hans Holbein the younger in the Tudor period, Sir Godfrey Kneller in the 17th century, Angelica Kaufmann (a founder member of the Royal Academy) and Johann Zoffany (a successful society portrait painter, buried at St Anne, Kew) in the 18th century.
- **musicians** – eg composers like Georg Frideric Händel and Johann Christian Bach ["The English Bach" youngest son of Johann Sebastian Bach]. Felix Mendelssohn taught Queen Victoria and her children music. Germans founded the Halle Orchestra and the Carl Rosa Opera Company and, more mundanely, there were many groups of itinerant German bands and street orchestras that enlivened the British Victorian and Edwardian street scene. Many of those street musicians came from the Palatinate (Pfalz) and John Willrich has written *The Wandering Musicians of the West Pfalz*, published by the Anglo-German FHS in 2003. John obtained a lot of the information for his book from the Musikantentum [ie Musicians Land] Museum at Bad Lichtenberg. Once again the area from which they came is quite small.

Many military bandsmen in the British Army were Germans or of German origin. It does seem that Germans benefitted from better musical education than was available in Britain. Friedrich Wilhelm Herschell, the astronomer, came here first as a musician in the Hanoverian Guards.

Obviously, in most jobs in the UK, Germans will have been in a minority but it does appear that in many cases – sugar, banking, music, baking, hairdressing – their importance was out of all proportion to their numbers in the population as a whole.

Internment

First World War

The First World War, and the anti-German hysteria that led up to it, largely destroyed the Victorian and Edwardian high tide of German immigration. The use of internment against all enemy alien males between 18 and 65, fully enforced after the sinking of the Lusitania in 1915, led to the break up of families. The accompanying deportation or repatriation of old people, and even some British-born wives and children, removed the remnants of the community. Even after the War when some families returned, it was still very unpopular to be, look or sound German and the community had not returned to its 19th century peak until recently. The trauma was such that, when the Anglo-German FHS was formed in the 1980s, some of the older members wanted their membership kept secret for fear of reprisals. Fortunately this is breaking down now and some members have even changed their surnames back to the German originals their grandparents tried to hide in 1914-19. Some of the best work on the anti-German hysteria has been written by Prof. Panikos Panayi eg *The Destruction of the German Communities in Britain during the First World War*, in *Germans in Britain since 1500*, ed by Panikos Panayi, published by The Hambledon Press, London, 1996. For the background see also: *German Immigrants in Britain during the Nineteenth Century, 1815-1914* by Panikos Panayi, published by Berg, Oxford, 1995.

The individual files of the First World War internees (usually known as "civilian POWs") have been largely destroyed by the Home Office though a few have been kept at TNA as examples. The surviving files do not hold a great amount of useful information so their destruction may not be as great a loss as we might have thought; except that we have no complete list of internees. There were lists of the internees produced by the British Government during the War: one copy for the "Protecting Power" to pass on to the enemy Government (ie Germany, Austria-Hungary, Bulgaria or Turkey), one for the Red Cross, and one to be kept by the British Government. The Red Cross copy is, we understand, complete but is now kept by the International Committee of the Red Cross (ICRC) in Geneva. As of mid 2011 the ICRC has ceased offering a research service as all their records of the First World War are being digitized with a view to their being made available to search online in 2014. It will probably be worth waiting for!

The British Government copy, so far as I have been able to ascertain, was kept at the Prisoner of War Information Bureau at Covent Garden in London where it was destroyed with all the other records in an air raid in WW2. Those records included millions of index cards and the records of the German- and Austrian-owned businesses that were confiscated at the outbreak of war. It was a very great loss for the history of the Germans in UK.

The Anglo-German FHS subsequently found a large number of lists in the Federal German Archives in Koblenz, copied them and has indexes available for searching (in the Names Index [qv]). However those lists only run from 1916 to 1919 and only relate to the changes in status of the internees; names and addresses, ages and places of birth, etc. do not appear in 99% of cases presumably because those details are on the earlier, missing, lists. They also include a list of those German civilian POWs for whom the Prisoner of War Information Bureau held property so that, after the War, those POWs could claim their property back. As I have already mentioned the POW Information Bureau records were all destroyed but the list is still useful. I should stress also that these are just for Germans and do not include Austrians, Bulgarians or Turks. Incidentally you do sometimes find post-war wills of Germans in the English wills indexes where the executor is the POW Information Bureau.

The Koblenz Archives do not know where the earlier lists are nor do the Home Office nor TNA. The Koblenz lists are probably the set forwarded to the German Government through the Protecting Power. From 1914 until she entered the War on the Allied side in 1917, that Protecting Power was the United States. After that the Protecting Power was Switzerland. There may well be some records in the Swiss Government Archives but inquiries have not, to date, been successful. There does not appear to be anything useful in the US Archives.

The main prison camps for Civilian POWs in the First World War were at Knockaloe and Douglas in the Isle of Man. There are few traces there today but the Isle of Man Museum and Archives in Douglas do have a representative collection of papers and artifacts. A book *Living with the Wire* was published in 1994 to accompany an exhibition put on at the Museum in Douglas and has now been republished in an edition with considerably more illustrations: It is available at the Museum and from the Anglo-German FHS bookshop.

There was a large number of internment and transit camps elsewhere in the UK. The main camp in London was at Alexandra Palace where the London POWs were collected and sorted before being moved to the Isle of Man. The Anglo-German FHS publishes: *Civilian Internment: An insight into Civilian Internment in Britain during WWI*, revised illustrated edition, 1998. It consists of the journal of an internee in the camps at Stratford, East London, and Alexandra Palace, by Richard Noschke, and an essay on conditions at Alexandra Palace written by another internee, Rudolph Rocker. Another Society member, John Walling, has written and privately published: *The Internment and Treatment of German Nationals during the 1st World War*. It is available from the Anglo-German FHS bookshop.

In 1998 the Anglo-German FHS unveiled a plaque to the First World War internees at the site of Knockaloe Camp and unveiled a similar plaque in 2000 at Alexandra Palace. A full list of First World War POW Camps in the British Empire, including their code letters as used in the Koblenz lists (above), was published at the time by the POW Information Bureau and has recently been reprinted by the Imperial War Museum: *Prisoners of War Information Bureau. List of Places of Internment*. It is available from the Imperial War Museum in London. There is also a list, as well as a useful chapter on German POWs in UK, in Sarah Paterson's *Tracing Your Prisoner of War Ancestors in the First World War. A Guide for Family Historians*, published by Pen & Sword, 2012.

The Postal History Society has published: *Prisoners of War in British Hands during WW1. A study of their history, the camps and their mails*. by Graham Marks, 2007. It provides a list of every camp known and a detailed history of several camps, both civilian and military, in the UK. There is also a new book about a camp in Northamptonshire: *Detained in England, 1914–20. Eastcote POW Camp, Pattishall*, by Colin R. Chapman and S. Richard Moss, published by Lochin Press.

Second World War
During the Second World War the fate of aliens was different. Civilian enemy aliens (including women) were arrested at the commencement of the war in September 1939, and many were transported to camps in Canada

Christmas 1916 postcard printed in Knockaloe camp.

and elsewhere. However, after the sinking of the SS "Arandora Star" by a U-boat in July 1940, with considerable loss of life, internees were kept in camps in UK, including the Isle of Man. Because large numbers of the internees were Jewish and other refugees from Nazi oppression, internment tribunals were set up to separate Nazi sympathisers from the others. The record cards, dating from 1939 to 1947, are available on microfilm at TNA in Class HO396, and can be searched for by name in TNA's "Discovery" catalogue. Where the tribunal decided that the alien did not need to be interned, the full record card is available; where they were to be interned, the Tribunal's reasons are on the back of the card and you would need to apply to the Home Office for permission to see those details. The cards give many useful personal details including the date and specific place of birth. The "Discovery" catalogue also includes a small number of personal Home Office files on individual internees (HO214) and Foreign Office files on individual internees (FO916).

Living with the Wire covers internment in the Isle of Man during the Second World War too. Interest is also growing in internment in UK during and after the War when there were 1,500 camps holding half a million men (though mainly military POWs). Dr J. Anthony Hellen has written a very useful article outlining the history, geography and nature of the camps: *Temporary Settlements and Transient Populations. The Legacy of Britain's Prisoner of War Camps: 1940-1948*, (in "Erdkunde", Boss Verlag Kleve, 2000); you can download a copy of the article, in English, from the website: **www.erkunde.uni-bonn.de/archive/**. He was the consultant to the award-winning BBC2 TV programme *The Germans We Kept* in 2000 and he points out that English Heritage are now taking more interest in preserving surviving evidence of the camps.

On the English Heritage website **www.english-heritage.org.uk** is a study *Prisoner of War Camps (1939-1948). Project Report* by Roger J. C. Thomas, 2003, which lists all the then-known camp sites in the UK. One site, at Harperley, Camp 93, in County Durham, appeared on the BBC *Restoration* programme and has now been scheduled as an ancient monument – see the illustrated article: *Harperley POW Camp. Memories and Monuments* by Margaret R. Nieke, on the English Heritage website. Another POW camp, Eden Camp 83, at Malton in North Yorkshire, has been partially restored as a museum to "The People's War" (**www.edencamp.co.uk**). The British public also seems to be taking more of an interest in the Second World War POW camps in UK going by the number of new studies being published. In 2012, there has been an account of a camp at Huyton on Merseyside: *Civilian Internment in Britain during WW2: Huyton Camp. Eye-Witness Accounts* edited and introduced by Jennifer Taylor, for the Anglo-German FHS; a camp near Basildon in Essex: *German POW Camp 266 Langdon Hills* by Ken Porter & Stephen Wynn, published by ukunpublished.co.uk; and a camp near Colchester in Essex: *Camp 186. The Lost Town at Berechurch* by Ken Free, published by Amberley Books. This looks like a trend so keep an eye out for further local publications of this sort.

One major source that has not yet been much used is the Deutsche Dienstelle whose website is at **www.dd.wast.de**. They hold large numbers of records of German military personnel: Army and other military and paramilitary organisations for WW2, Prisoners of War, and also Naval personnel 1871-1947. Normally they will only make the information known to close relatives but it is always worth asking.

If you still do not know where they came from...

If, even after checking in the sources outlined above, you still do not know where your immigrant ancestor came from, there are some ways in which you can narrow the field of search.

Names

The German system of **first names** can often be confusing to British people. While most British people had only one first name until the end of the 19th century, Germans had two names and sometimes more. You often find brothers called Johann Heinrich, Johann Friedrich and Johann August! They would not have been called Johann or John in Germany but Heinrich, Friedrich or August. This system did not transfer to UK very well and immigrants may have suddenly found themselves being called John. British officials expected people to have only one name and so often omitted the second name in official documents, or abbreviated it to an initial letter. So your August Schmidt might be listed in the censuses or the civil registration indexes as "Johann A Schmidt". Sometimes the immigrant worked out what was happening and transposed his names or dropped the one he did not want to use but in many cases they just went along with their "new" name. This is something you must consider – possibly the first name you have is not the one the immigrant arrived with.

Like English **surnames**, German surnames can be very localised and can provide the clue you need to trace your immigrant ancestor. For example the German for butcher varies considerably: in the northwest it is Schlachter, in the northeast Fleischer, in the southwest Metzger and in the southeast Fleischhacker. If you think that your German surname is unusual it is worth looking in a German surname dictionary in case it is predominantly from a single area.

A factor that often throws newcomers to German research is that, in some cases, the surname of a wife or daughter is given the feminine ending "-in". Thus Rocker becomes Rockerin, Müller becomes Müllerin and Treuten becomes Treutenin. Where the surname already ends in "-in", "er" is inserted instead so that Schwecklin becomes Schwecklerin. These changes to the form of surnames are, however, not common in present-day Germany.

The most helpful German surname dictionaries are: *Etymologisches Wörterbuch der Deutschen Familiennamen* by Prof. J K Brechenmacher,

2 vols, C A Starke-Verlag, Limburg a.d.Lahn, (n.d.), (this is the German surname dictionary that covers most names but its coverage concentrates more on Southern Germany; the coverage of Northern Germany is less complete); and *Deutsches Namenlexikon* by Hans Bahlow, Suhrkamp Taschenbuch Verlag, 1985, (this is just one volume and so is less complete but is better for northern German surnames). Hans Bahlow's dictionary is also available in English as *A Dictionary of German Surnames* translated and revised by Edda Gentry, published by the Max Kade Institute for German-American Studies, University of Wisconsin, second edition, 2002. Duden, the German dictionary publisher, also publishes *Familiennamen. Herkunft und Bedeutung von 20,000 Nachnamen*, by Rosa & Volker Kohlheim, 2000 [ie *Family Names. Origin and Meaning of 20,000 Surnames*]. The Anglo-German FHS has copies of these books.

A very peculiar naming system that occurred in parts of North West Germany (mainly western Hanover, northern Westphalia, Oldenburg and Lippe-Detmold) involved **farm surnames**. From about the year 1000 to about 1840, under the form of the feudal system in operation there, people who lived on certain farms, called Hof, took the farm surname. Each Hof generated a specific surname. The farmer took that name when he took over the farm, dropping his original surname. The Hof was inherited by the youngest son or, failing sons, the youngest daughter. They retained their surname – the Hof name. Other sons had to move out and lost their Hof surname when they did so. With luck they could marry a Hof heiress on another Hof and so take her Hof surname. If not they often went back to the family's original pre-Hof surname, lost possibly several generations earlier. So a Hof could carry the surname Richter; if a son of the Hof had to leave and married the heiress of the Hof Meyer zu Uphausen, he and his children took the surname Mayer zu Uphausen instead of Richter. Emigrants, however, could well bring the Hof surname with them to their new country. The best description of the system in English is in an article: *Surname Changes in Northwestern Germany* by Roger P. Minert, *German Genealogical Digest*, Vol. 16, No 1, Spring 2000. The Anglo-German FHS has a copy.

Telephone Directories

The old German phone books were not easy to consult and are thankfully a thing of the past. People's names were organized alphabetically by town or city so you had to know which town or city to search. Now you can do it online. One of the best websites at present is **http//home.meinestadt. de/deutschland/verzeichnis**. In it you can search in "Das Telefonbuch" and find the telephone number and address. Though you still have to choose a place ("Ort").

If you find that the surname seems to be restricted to a locality, it may be worth writing to the local City or Town Hall and seeing what happens. This has been fruitful in the past: an immigrant called August Trepte was stated in the 1851 census to be born in Saxony – rather a large place at the time! Looking in the telephone book the surname was found to be most common around Leipzig. Even though the immigrant probably arrived in London in the 1830s, a fax was sent to the City Archives (Stadtarchiv) in Leipzig who, by return, sent full details of the family being sought. This would, of course, only work with a relatively rare and localised surname. Incidentally the Christian name "August" would have suggested Saxony anyway as it was the name of many of the Kings of Saxony.

Another use of telephone directories, especially where the immigrant arrived in the last 100 to 150 years, is to obtain addresses of other people with the same surname and write to them. This has provided the big breakthrough in several cases that I know of but again is only really practicable if you know the region of origin and the surname is rare, or localised enough, for the numbers to be manageable.

Genealogical Dictionaries

It is not true that, where a surname starts with "von", it generally means that the family was ennobled. In many cases it is just a locative surname. However, when a person was ennobled in Germany they normally added a "von" to their surname so it could be a pointer. Also the surname does not have to be a placename; "von" could be put in front of any surname – you could even have von Schmidt! It does, however, mean that they may be listed in one of the various books on the German nobility. Incidentally the old nobility normally abbreviate "von" to "v." to differentiate themselves from "modern" nobility.

The official status of the nobility in the German Empire was abolished in 1919 but the titles still continue in use. The main degrees of nobility were: König (King), Elector (a ruler with a vote in the election of the Holy Roman Emperor), Fürst (Prince), Grossherzog (Grand Duke), Herzog

(Duke), Graf (Count or Earl), Freiherr (Baron) and Reichsritter (Imperial knight).

There are several different series of genealogical dictionaries of the German nobility and what we would call the landed gentry. I fear that the overall system is very confusing! I will try to simplify it!

The German version of the *Almanac de Gotha*, the *Gothaischen Genealogischen Hofkalendar* [*Gotha Genealogical Court Calendar*] published between 1785 and 1944, gives the pedigrees of the ruling houses of countries that were or had been part of the Holy Roman Empire: ie the German Empire, the Austrian Empire, the Netherlands, Belgium, Luxemburg, and parts of Italy, France, Switzerland, Poland and the Ukraine. It lists most of the higher nobility but most of the mere "von" families do not appear.

The *Genealogisches Handbuch des Adels* [ie *The Genealogical Handbook of the Nobility*], which is in 152 volumes, covers a larger number of families. Publication started in 1951 and still continues. There are separate series of volumes for Fürstliche (princely or royal lineages); Gräfliche (lineages of Counts – equivalent to British Earls); Freiherrliche (barons) and Adelige (nobility without a title). The Anglo-German FHS holds a large number of the volumes and there is a printed index covering up to volume 150.

An alphabetical series called the *Adelslexikon* [*Lexicon of the Nobility*] was published between 1972 and 2005. It consists of 16 volumes from A to Z and a supplementary 17th volume. The 18th volume is a complete index to that series. It includes all proven noble families, except those extinct before 1800, and puts special emphasis on families ennobled after 1850. The Adelslexikon however, is included as part of the Genealogisches Handbuch des Adels and numbered in that sequence not in a separate Adelslexikon sequence! There is a complete set of the Genealogisches Handbuch des Adels on the open shelves of the Humanities I Reading Room of the British Library at St Pancras. While it is in German, it is set out much like the Burke's *Peerage*, the format is easy to understand and each volume contains its own index.

Another series is the *Deutsches Geschlechterbuch* or *German Lineage Book*, which began publication in 1889. This is more equivalent to the Landed Gentry – it covers Bürgerlich families ie commoners – but the volumes are often geographically-based ie there are 5 volumes for Baden,

1 for the Baltic States, 3 for Brandenburg, etc. By 2007 a total of 219 volumes had been published. A full surname index to volumes 1 to 209 has been published and the publishers now publish back volumes on CD-ROM (volumes 1 to 167, had been published by 2012). The Anglo-German FHS is subscribing to the CD-ROM series and can make searches for members.

All these series are published by one firm: C. A. Starke Verlag of Limburg an der Lahn, and on their website is the Starke Genealogy Index of German Nobility (**www.rootsweb.ancestry.com/~autwgw/ sgi/index-htm**) which covers the Genealogisches Handbuch des Adels series. Another useful online source created by Paul Theroff is at **www. angelfire.com/realm/gotha/gotha/gotha.htm**. It incorporates pedigrees from various published works covering European nobility including Gotha and the Genealogisches Handbuch des Adels.

Coats of Arms (Wappen)

The German for coats of arms is "Wappen". There are several publications that list and show German coats of arms, besides the Genealogical Dictionaries described above, and many claim a connection with a Johann Siebmacher of Nuremburg who died in 1611. He published a book of coats of arms, *Wappenbuch*, in 1605 and there have been countless editions since then. Again there is an index that covers all of them: *General-Index zu den Siebmacher'schen Wappenbüchern, 1605-1961* by Hanns Jäger-Sunstenau, published by Akademische Druck und Verlagsanstalt, Graz, Austria, 1964. There is a set in the Rare Books reading room in the British Library. These cover coats of arms of the German and Austrian Empires and even areas like the Baltic lands which were in neither.

You should be able to search to see if there is a coat of arms for your family online. In **www.ancestry.co.uk** you can search Siebmacher's Wappenbuch by surname. If you find an entry, the text in Siebmacher usually gives a potted history of the family concerned though there is not always an illustration of the coat of arms. In some cases, like the v. Müthel family of Appelsee in Livland, now in Estonia, it says "Wappen?" implying that the editors thought that the family was entitled to arms but could find no record of it. That makes the index all the more helpful as it obviously includes families which do not have proven arms. What you see are digital copies of the relevant pages. You can also search in **www.**

wappenbuch.com, which gives black and white illustrations of the arms and **www.wappenbuch.de** which gives colour pictures. And very pretty some of them are too!

Unlike English arms it appears that coats of arms can be borne undifferenced by several members of one family at the same time and the designs often seem (to English eyes) unusually pictorial. Also the blazon is commonly in plain German rather than the Norman-French we are used to. As there was no single country covering Germany, there were several different organizations that controlled the use of arms in different places. Because of that the records may be in different places. There is no single authority like the College of Arms for England and Wales or the Lord Lyons Court for Scotland. However, the Holy Roman Empire did exist as an overall authority until it was abolished by Napoleon and so many records will be in the relevant archives in Vienna.

If you cannot get your hands on one of these German publications, a useful source covering all Europe is Rietstap's Armorial: *Armorial Général* by J B Reitstap, (2 volumes, 2nd edition, 1885, reprinted by Heraldry Today, 1965; 11 Supplementary volumes also reprinted by Heraldry Today 1965-6; 6 volumes of illustrations reprinted in 3 volumes by Heraldry Today, 1967). A complete set is in the Society of Genealogists Library and many large reference libraries should have a set. It lists the armorial families in alphabetical order and, in a separate volume, illustrates the arms.

Auswanderer or German Emigrant records

In most German States an individual was not free to leave the State without permission. Before leaving they were supposed to seek leave in writing from the local ruler. Young men had to show that they had done their compulsory national service (generally between the ages of 17 and 21), that they were not leaving behind dependents (eg parents, wives or children) who might become chargeable to the State in the future, and that they had settled all their debts (and could prove it!). As you can imagine these applications could give rise to a lot of useful genealogical information. Many of these records have been indexed and the relevant archives may hold those indexes.

In some cases, such as Württemberg, the indexes have been published. Württemberg emigrants from about 1820 to 1914 are listed in the eight volumes of *The Württemberg Emigration Index*. The Anglo-German FHS has the first seven volumes but it is now searchable online at **www.ancestry.co.uk**. It provides the parish of birth and the date of emigration also a reference to the original records held in the Baden-Württemberg State Archives at Ludwigsburg, which usually contain several pages of records relating to each individual. NB these documents relate to the Kingdom of Württemberg not the present Land of Baden-Württemberg.

There are several other similar published lists covering eg the former Duchy of Brunswick and the former Prussian province of Westphalia and the LDS Church has copies of some of the indexes of the former Grand Duchy of Baden. If you know the State the immigrant came from, you could write to see if there is such an index. Most archives in Germany appear to have records of "Auswanderung" [ie Emigration] but they are not much use without an index unless you know where the emigrant came from.

In the 1990s the Land of Lower Saxony (Niedersächsen) funded an index of all emigrants from the former States that are now part of their Land covering 1753 to the 1930s. Unfortunately, they decided to include only those emigrants who left Europe for America, Australia, India, etc.; it does not normally include those who just moved within Europe and so emigrants to the UK are omitted. This is annoying but it might still be worth checking in the index as many emigrants possibly intended to go to America but got no further than England! You can now search it online at the Lower Saxony State Archives (Niedersächsen Landesarchiv) website: **aidaonline.niedersachsen.de**.

Of course, many could not meet the criteria to be allowed to leave, or did not think it worth risking being refused. They slipped away without asking. In many cases, however, there may well be indexes which include them too – when they failed to appear for their military service, or it was otherwise noticed that they had left, their names might be published in the local newspapers as deserters and these too may well have been indexed. Those who slipped away illegally and did not turn up to fulfil their military service will, in many cases, have forfeited their German State citizenship. This might explain the German people who claim to be of no citizenship when eg they naturalize.

German Passenger Lists

The most significant surviving sets of records of emigrants departing from Germany by ship are the Hamburg Passenger Lists. These cover passengers leaving the port of **Hamburg** between 1850 and 1934 – nearly 6 million entries. The details from the original ships' lists include: age, occupation, marital status, city of origin, and the name of the ship and its destination and date of sailing. These are now most conveniently searchable on **www.ancestry.co.uk**. The lists for 1850-54 are in alphabetical order so there is no need for an index. After 1854 there are two main series with separate (usually annual) indexes: Direct Lists (where the ship went from Hamburg to America or elsewhere outside Europe without any intermediate stops) 1854-1934; and Indirect Lists (where the ship made an intermediate stop) 1854-1910. The latter lists are, of course, of more use to those looking for Germans who ended up in the UK. Hamburg was one of the main ports for German emigration at this period, especially from north Germany, and many ships went from there to the UK, to North America and even to Australasia.

However, there were other German emigration ports including several on the Baltic like Danzig (now Gdansk in Poland), Stettin (now Szczecin in Poland), and even Königsberg (now Kaliningrad in Russia). The emigration trade through these Baltic ports was relatively small and I know of few records of emigrants. I understand that passenger lists for **Stettin** survive for 1869-1898 in the archives at Greifswald (Vorpommersches Landesarchiv Greifswald).

The most important other German emigration port was **Bremen** and, because the river Weser was silting up, the new port of **Bremerhaven** on the North Sea coast after 1830. Both Bremerhaven and Hamburg have Emigration Museums but the Germans themselves consider the former to be far superior. The official records of emigration from Bremen and Bremerhaven were routinely destroyed after three years and those that survive only cover 1920-23 and 1924-39. They have been indexed and can be searched online gratis at the website of the local Bremen family history society Die Maus (ie The Mouse) at **www.die.maus-bremen.de**. Their "Auswanderung" database, however, also includes a large number of earlier emigration records taken from local newspapers, some surviving ships' passenger lists and other miscellaneous sources. There are other Bremen Passenger Lists available online and in printed form but, so far as I can tell, these were compiled from the American port records of incoming immigrants. They will not include those who disembarked in UK.

Of course some emigrants from Germany found it more convenient to use other ports such as Antwerp in Belgium; Rotterdam in the Netherlands; and Le Havre in France.

For **Antwerp** the only surviving emigration lists are the embarkation lists of 1855, published in Salt Lake City as *The Antwerp Emigration Index*, edited by Charles M Hall, (no date). For **Rotterdam** the archives, relating to shipping including passenger and emigration lists, were destroyed in WW2. The Palatine emigration lists of 1709 (already mentioned) do survive but they were in the British Treasury records held in London.

Many emigrants from southern Germany left through **Le Havre** 1830-70. There are, however, no surviving lists of emigrants; only incomplete lists of crews and passengers on some cargo vessels. The LDS Church has filmed the Le Havre commercial cargo vessel passenger lists for the years 1750 to 1886 and these are available in the LDS Library.

PART II:
Tracing German Ancestors in the German-speaking parts of Europe

In what follows, I try to give a helpful overview of the kind of records that are likely to be available in most areas that are, or were formerly, parts of Germany. I refer you to the Introduction for an explanation of the political and geographical problems.

There are several publications available that give the addresses of archives, civil registration offices and Family History Societies and that go into more detail than is possible here about the local arrangements for consulting archives. The most detailed book currently available is *The German Research Companion* by Shirley J. Riemer, Roger P. Minert & Jennifer A. Anderson, published by Lorelei Press, P O Box 221356, Sacramento, CA 95822-8356, USA, 3rd edition 2010. This volume concentrates on 1871-1945 Germany but provides a great amount of useful details on research there. It does, however, have a strong American bias and contains much on research in USA. A slimmer volume that consists principally of addresses is *Useful Addresses*, edited by Peter & Jenny Towey, Anglo-German FHS Research Guide Four, 6th edition, 2011. It covers Austria and other parts of the former German, Austrian and Russian Empires too. It also provides addresses of the many family history societies known to exist in Germany. As their publications are normally in German, it is not worth joining unless you can read at least some of their magazines, etc. However it might be worth your while to join the local society covering the area from which your ancestor came and learn enough German to use their services. There are also several societies based in North America which publish in English and are a great resource for English-speakers. These are also listed but check out the website of the Federation of Eastern European Family History Societies (FEEFHS) (**feefhs.org**) of which most such societies are members.

However, the most up-to-date source for this kind of information is now the Internet. A good place to start is the webpage of the German Genealogy Computer Society (Verein für Computergenealogie) at **www.genealogy.**

net which provides access to many useful websites and contains many large databases. While the main site is in German, this website address will take you through to an English language version. It contains links to the webpages of the German genealogy societies, several large databases and articles on research in other German-speaking parts of Europe.

I would also recommend the website of ProGenealogists, a US-based group of professional genealogists who share a lot of their expertise online at **www.progenealogists.com/germany/**. Here you will find articles on research in different areas of Germany and links to other sites. They also have webpages for research in Denmark, Hungary, Poland, Romania, Slovakia and Switzerland.

Do not forget Cyndi's List at **www.cyndislist.com**. It is a comprehensive portal site for all kinds of sources for research in different countries. The site does have a North American bias but there is still a great deal for non-North Americans. The sections on Germany and other European countries will open your eyes to the vast number of different, and often new, sources that there are out there. Keep up to date!

German Historical Geography

As mentioned in the Introduction, Germany did not become a single state until 1871 (and even then did not include German-speaking areas like Austria). Before then there were many separate States and their names, boundaries and alliances changed frequently over the centuries. You cannot take a snapshot of the political situation at some time in the past and say that that is the "original" form. That is why you need good maps of the area you are interested in and an idea of the history of the area. There are some published books and articles in English but you may have to obtain a good German-language history of your area and translate it! Look out for old, pre-1914, school atlases which can often be found cheaply in second-hand bookshops. You can do research in Germany without knowing any German but you will do much better if you learn to read and write a bit.

Lands of the German Empire and Before by Wendy K. Uncapher, published by Origins, 4327 Milton Avenue, Janesville, WI 53546, USA, 2nd edition, February 2004, gives useful histories and "timelines" of the

German Empire and of its constituent parts, with outline maps showing the boundaries and the Counties (Kreis) or other equivalent divisions. A particularly helpful feature is mapping the various political bodies that covered "Germany" over the last 1,000 years, like the Holy Roman Empire, the Confederation of the Rhine, the North German Confederation, the German Empire and the Weimar Republic. The book is available in the UK from the Anglo-German FHS bookshop. Do not forget that the boundaries of the country we know as Germany today – see map – were only settled in 1990!

You can also search for information on individual places online in your preferred search engine. The Wikipedia entries are often helpful but not always reliable. You may need to try several different sources before you will be sure that you understand the history of a place.

One of the major problems is that there are often several different places with the same or a similar name in the country at any one time. I was looking for a place near Bremen called Osterholz, the birthplace in about the mid-19th century of a sugarbaker in London. The usual sources directed me to Osterholz-Scharmbeck a small town some miles north of Bremen. That resulted in a lot of wasted time and money as I had the parish registers of that Osterholz searched and found nothing.

The best gazetteer for the German Empire as it existed 1871-1918, its fullest extent, is *Meyers Orts- und Verkehrs-Lexikon des Deutschen Reichs*, the 1912 edition of which is now available in a 3-volume set, edited by Raymond S. Wright III. The Anglo-German FHS has a set. You can find it online in **www.ancestry.com** in their card catalogue and search by place name. One problem however, besides the Gothic script, is that you really need access to another publication to make a lot of sense of the highly-abbreviated entries: *How to Read & Understand Meyers Orts- und Verkehrs-Lexikon des Deutschen Reiches* by Wendy K. Uncapher, published by Origins, 1521 E. Racine St (Hwy. 11), Janesville, WI 53546, USA, 2003. It contains detailed instructions in English on how to interpret the entries. It is well worth obtaining a copy if you are seriously intending to research in Germany during the time of the German Empire. The Anglo-German FHS has a copy.

When I looked for Osterholz in Meyer's I found that there was another place of that name which was a suburb of Bremen itself. It was not a separate parish but was called Osterholz bei Hemelingen to differentiate

The Lands of present-day Germany.

it. That proved to be the right place. We were lucky that we knew roughly where it was in Germany as there were several other places of the same name.

Records filmed by the LDS Church

If you cannot get to Germany very easily, do not fret. The LDS Church has been microfilming archives from the German-speaking parts of Europe for decades and there are vast collections of those microfilms in Salt Lake City from where they can be ordered in the usual way via your local LDS Church Family History Library. The microfilming does not just cover parish registers, though large numbers of them have been filmed, but police records, passenger lists, censuses, court records, land records and many printed books.

The best place to start is the LDS Church genealogy website **www.familysearch.org**. The latest version of this website allows you to search in the old International Genealogical Index (IGI) but also in a lot of new German and other records online. There are an increasing number of records there which are not indexed but in which you can search page by page as you would in an unindexed parish register. If you do not have access to a personal computer, you can always access their records online at your local LDS Church Library which should be in your local telephone directory.

If you want to know what other records and books the LDS Church might have microfilmed from the area you are interested in, look for the "Catalog"; then "Place Names", and insert the place name in the search box.

The German Alphabet

This is as good a time as any to introduce one of the main difficulties involved in research in Germany: the alphabet. Before the end of the Second World War, German was written in a different alphabet. Many of you will be familiar with the printed "Gothic", "Fraktur" or "black letter" form. The equivalent handwritten form is, alas, equally difficult to read until you become used to it – see the alphabet on page 64. But do not let me put you off. It is no different from learning to read eg English 17th century handwriting and the technique for learning it is much the same: practice, practice and more practice! There is a useful bilingual book called: *The German Script*, published by Verlag Degener & Co, Nürnberger Strasse 27, D-91413 Neustadt a.d. Aisch, Germany. Many also swear by the late Edna M. Bentz's book: *If I Can, You Can Decipher Germanic Records*. Anyone seriously intending to do research in German records before 1945 should get a copy of one or the other. As a general rule, Roman Catholic records in Germany are written in Latin in italic script which is similar to the alphabet we use; such records are therefore much easier to use (so long as Latin is not a problem for you!).

Civil Registration

Civil Registration did not cover the whole of the then German Empire until 1876. Even then the records were not kept centrally but in the local civil registry office: the "Standesamt" of the area; often this is physically in the Town Hall or "Rathaus". For some parts of Germany, civil registration started earlier: Prussia and most of the Eastern provinces started in 1874; some former states that were conquered by the French during the Revolutionary and Napoleonic Wars, like Alsace-Lorraine (Elsaß-Lothringen), the Rhineland, the Palatinate (Pfalz) and Baden, started in 1792; Westphalia began in 1808; Hanover in 1809; and Bremen and Oldenburg in 1811. Once you know the area that your ancestor came from, you need to do some further research to find out when civil registration started locally. The map on pages 66 and 67 gives you an outline to start from.

To obtain birth, marriage or death certificates, therefore, you need to know where, and roughly when, the event took place. If you know, you should write (preferably in German) to:

**Standesamt,
[postcode], [name of the town],
Germany**.

An alphabet of the Old German script.

Postcodes are particularly important when you write to Germany. The postcode is a 5 digit number and can be obtained from a publication called: "Postleitzahlenbuch" (or Postcode book). NB the postcodes changed in 1993 so do not use any postcodes from before that date. With the Internet the best course is to Google "Standesamt [name of place]" and note the address. You will often find an e-mail address to save you writing a letter.

If the event took place in a small village, which may not have had its own Standesamt, you will need to find the appropriate Standesamt probably in a nearby town or village by using Meyer's Gazetteer (see page 60).

In a large city like Berlin or Hamburg there are likely to be several Standesamts and you will need to find the right one if you can. In some cases the 19th century City is now the central area of the current City and is called "Mitte". The Standesamt covering that old city (which is often the area you are interested in) is eg "Hamburg Mitte" and that is where you should write. Otherwise find the address of the City Rathaus and use the same postal code. If you do not write German, there are a number of publications which give draft letters in German so that you only need to fill in the blanks with names and dates! Don't forget though that you will still have to be able to read the reply when it arrives. Some members of the Anglo-German FHS offer to help other members with translations.

The Anglo-German FHS publishes *Tracing Your German Ancestors*, Research Guide 2, Anglo-German FHS, 6th ed. 2009, which contains draft letters in German (with translations) that members have used and found helpful in the past.

The Civil Registration records in Germany are not as accessible to the public as the British equivalents are. Indeed, until recently only proven direct descendants were entitled to see their ancestors' birth, marriage or death certificates and there are no publicly-available indexes to civil registration. A law, passed in February 2007, makes civil registration records more accessible for family history research. Since 1 January 2009 the records are accessible to researchers: for births after: 110 years; marriages: 80 years; deaths: 30 years. Proof of a direct relationship to the subject of the record sought will only be required in cases where the set time period has not yet elapsed. Even then, the record may be accessible if it can be shown that all "participating parties" have died at least 30 years ago. Participating parties in a birth record are both parents and the child, and both spouses in a marriage. Special regulations apply to records of adoptees.

This seems like good news for researchers. However, in many cases the newly "public" records are being transferred to the local archives as the Standesamt does not have room to provide public access. The large influx of new material caused problems for some archives and each year more records will arrive. There is also the problem of finding-aids. Each Standesamt has had individual problems and it is worth contacting

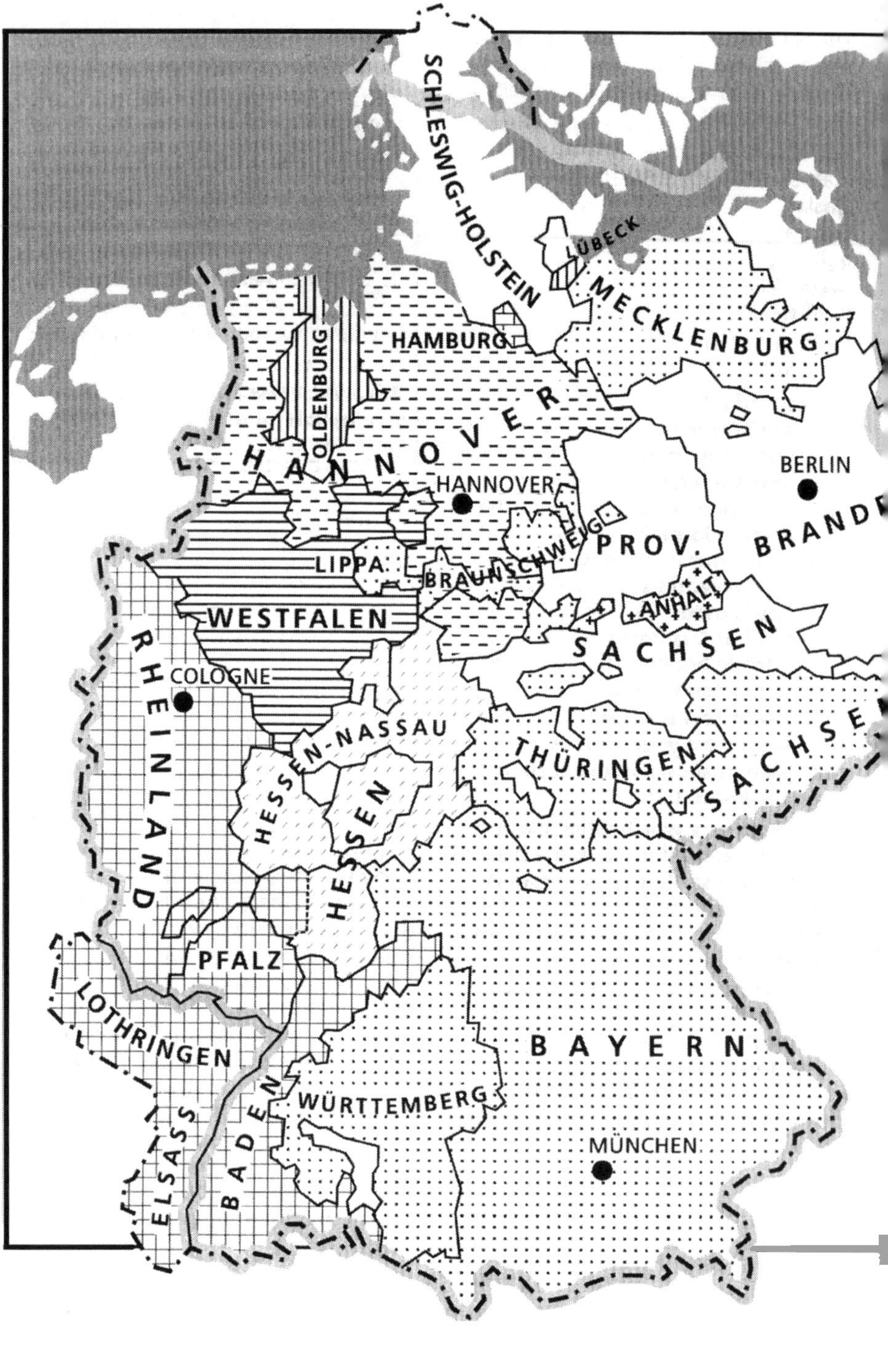

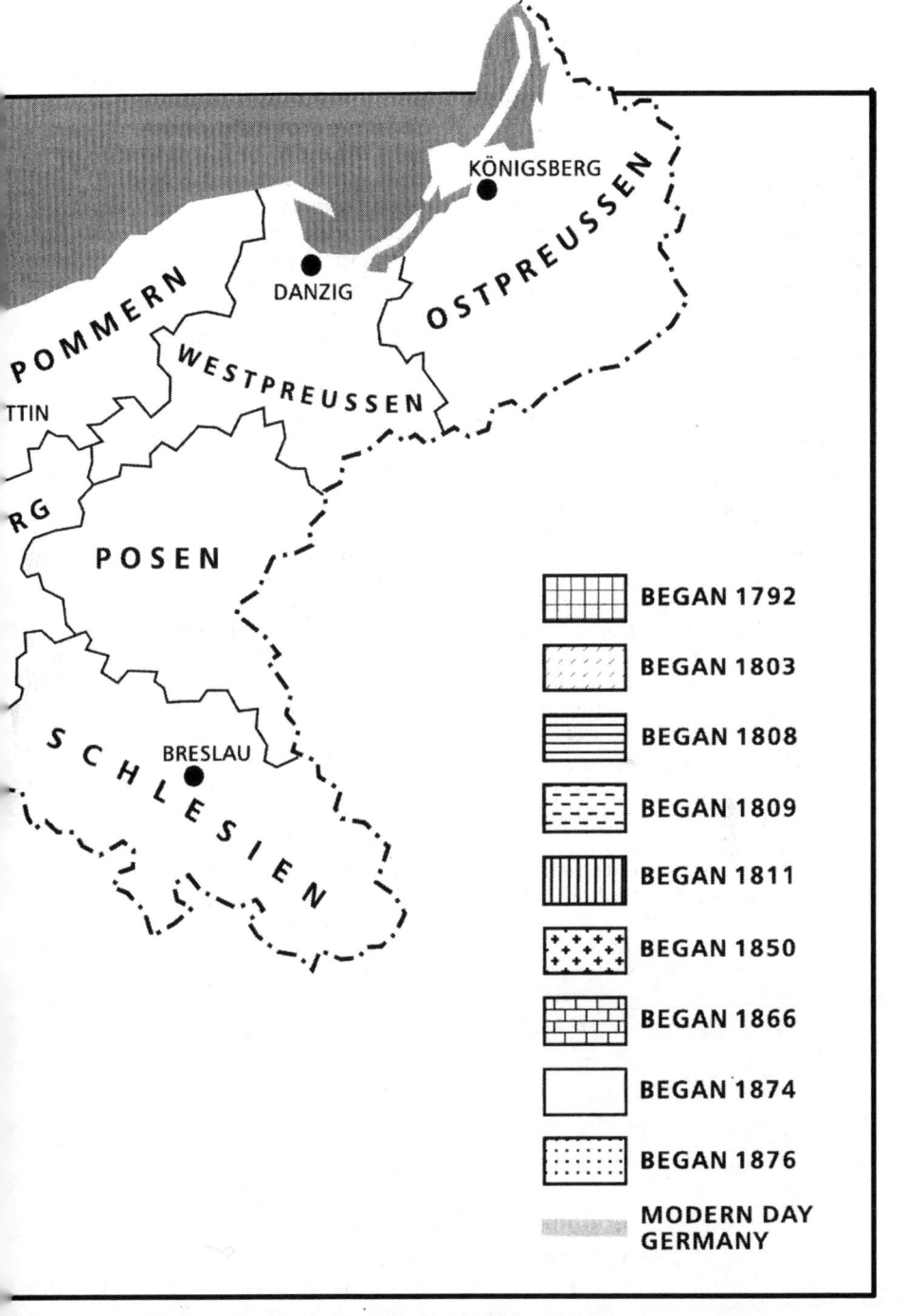

Legend	Date
▦	BEGAN 1792
▨	BEGAN 1803
▤	BEGAN 1808
▦	BEGAN 1809
▥	BEGAN 1811
✛	BEGAN 1850
▦	BEGAN 1866
☐	BEGAN 1874
⁙	BEGAN 1876
▓	MODERN DAY GERMANY

Regions shown: POMMERN, WESTPREUSSEN, OSTPREUSSEN, POSEN, SCHLESIEN
Cities: KÖNIGSBERG, DANZIG, BRESLAU, (STE)TTIN, (BERG?) RG

Map of German Empire 1871–1919 showing dates when civil registration started.

the Standesamt or local archive first to discover how the system works locally.

Another complication is in paying for the certificates. In the past, when you were only allowed to receive the certificate because you were a close family member, the official often provided you with a copy gratis. However, the newly publicly-available certificates are like other public records and as such there is likely to be a fee. This will depend on the rules of the individual archives and you will just have to ask. Do not send any money until you are asked. They will require an electronic bank transfer into their archive's bank account. Within Germany and most other parts of the Eurozone, such bank transfers are free as they are within UK. However, to transfer money by electronic transfer from UK to Germany is very expensive, especially when the cost of the certificate itself is likely to be only a few Euros. British banks I have dealt with charge between £9 and £14 for such a small transaction. So if you can order several certificates at one go it will make it seem less expensive. Otherwise, you can do as I do and pretend that the bank charge is part of the cost of the certificate!

If you are not completely certain that the person whose certificate you want is your direct ancestor and the certificate is too recent to benefit from the new legislation, I suggest that you apply in the usual way and see what happens. As you are ordering the record because you believe you are a relative, the officials in the Standesamt may well be willing to give you the benefit of the doubt, but don't count on it. If you are reasonably sure, an assertion that you are a direct descendant of the person whose certificate you are ordering, and a draft family tree showing the relationship, should be adequate.

If you are having difficulty in obtaining a certificate, you may decide to look for the church registration of baptism, marriage or burial instead (see Church Registers below). The churches are less likely to consider themselves to be covered by the privacy laws.

The information you get on civil registration certificates varies from State to State and from time to time but, generally speaking, you get more useful data than you get in the equivalent English, Welsh or Irish certificates. It also has the advantage over the church registers that, as the form itself is printed and the individual information is sometimes typed, it is easier to read. Where the areas' civil registration records start in 1792 the records are very detailed and follow the form of the French certificates of the period.

As the public does not have access to the civil registration indexes (except those certificatesthat have recently become accessible and for which indexes are presumably being prepared) and as they are all held locally, it is very unlikely that any national or even regional birth, marriage or death indexes will be available online in the foreseeable future.

However it is possible that the older registers themselves might be put online without an index which would be better than waiting for an index. For example the Landesarchiv (State Archive) Baden-Württemberg has digitized and put online the civil birth, marriage and death records 1810-70 for the former **Grand Duchy of Baden** held in the sub-archive at Freiburg im Breisgau. They are not indexed but, if you know roughly when and where an ancestor was born, married or died there, it would be worth a search. The quality of the pictures is excellent and you can print them or download them gratis. Indeed you are not allowed to see the original records in the archives any more – which is good for the records and saves you a trip!

To access them go to the Landesarchiv Baden-Württemberg website **www2.landesarchiv-bw.de** and choose "Staatsarchiv Freiburg". On the left hand side of the screen choose "Bestände & Bestellung"; then "List der Online-Findbüchern". In "Findbuchliste" choose "L. Selekte"; then choose "L 10 Standesbücher" which will take you through to a list of Amtsgerichten (District Courts) in alphabetical order with dates. Each Amtsgericht includes, in alphabetical order, each place within the district and you can then click on the place, religion and dates you are interested in, which will take you through to the digitised registers. These are the civil records produced between 1810, when Baden, as an ally of Republican France, introduced the French style system, and 1870, the year before Baden joined the German Empire.

Many more such digitised records are becoming available online. You just have to find them.

Church Registers

Once you have got back before Civil Registration, or if you cannot obtain the certificate, the next major source for Christians is the "Kirchenbücher", church books or registers. I find that the best guide to the church registers available in English is *German Church Books. Beyond the Basics* by Kenneth L. Smith, published by Picton Press, Camden, Maine, ME 04843-1111, USA. It provides detailed descriptions of the information you can find in the registers with advice on how to solve genealogical problems. Any serious researcher should get a copy.

As a general rule, the registers start in the 16th or 17th centuries and continue through to the present day. Also they contain considerably more information that you could hope to find in the equivalent British registers. There were three main Christian denominations in the German-speaking areas: Roman Catholic, Lutheran or Evangelical and Reformed Lutheran or Calvinist churches. Each kept registers which are held either in the parish, in the Town or City Archives (Stadtarchiv), in the State Archives (Staatsarchiv) or have been gathered together into special church archives. For detailed lists and addresses consult the Anglo-German FHS's *Useful Addresses* and *The German Research Companion*.

The main types of German Church records of use to family historians are:

- Baptism register – *Taufregister*: The entries normally provide the child's name, date and place of baptism, date of birth, mother's name, name, residence and occupation of father, name and occupation of mother's father, names and residences of witnesses or godparents. Many provide even more useful information.
- Confirmations – *Konfirmation*: Children in the Roman Catholic and Protestant churches were usually confirmed between 11 and 16 years of age. These registers are more common in Germany than in England and can often provide additional information about the family a decade or so after the birth.
- Marriage register – *Trauregister*: These normally give the date & place of the marriage, name, age, residence & occupation of the groom, the name & age of the bride, the names of bride's and groom's parents, their residences and (the fathers') occupations, the name and date of

death of the previous spouse if either party was widowed, and the names, residences & occupations of the witnesses.
- Death register – *Sterberegister*: These usually give the name, occupation, age at death, date & place of death and of burial, and the names of surviving spouse and children. Sometimes the cause of death is also given.
- Burial register – *Begräbnisse*: These normally give the name of the deceased, their age at death, residence, occupation, dates and places of death and burial, cause of death and the names of any surviving spouse. Sometimes the gravestone inscription is also given – very useful where, as is often the case in Germany, the grave plots are cleared and re-used every 30 years or so.

The records of the former **Deutsche Zentralstelle für Genealogie (DZfG)(German Central Office for Genealogy)** were incorporated into the Saxon State Archive (Sächsische Staatsarchiv) in Leipzig in 1995. It had been the German national genealogy collection. They have been collecting material on genealogy since the beginning of the 20th century and one of their main sources is a slip index, (the "ASTAKA" or "Ahnenstammkartei") of over a million slips, which indexes manuscript and printed family histories (including articles in books and magazines) in the DZfG collection. Though I understand that it has not been added to since 1995, it is well worth a search, just in case your family has already been researched. The LDS Church has microfilmed the slip index but the organisation of the slips (a form of Soundex based on the local German pronunciation) is so complex that you need a book to discover which film to order. You can write to the DZfG in German to ask if your German family is covered. Their reply will be in German. This will only work if the surname is uncommon in Germany or you know in which town or village in Germany the family were living. As they have access to the slip index and know how to use it, it would be much quicker to get them to do a search than to attempt it yourself. Their address is

Sächsisches Staatsarchiv,
Staatsarchiv Leipzig,
Schongauerstrasse 1,
D-04329 Leipzig,

Germany
Website: www.archiv.sachsen.de

The building is at the end of a tram route from central Leipzig and you should always book yourself in in advance if you are going in person. You cannot rely on finding English-speaking members of staff to help you when you get there – but do ask when you book.

The DZfG collection also includes copies of German parish registers made from 1935 to 1945 as part of the Nazi Government Department, the Reichsippenamt's policy of preserving genealogical material. They have published 3 volumes listing the registers and these volumes are available for sale at the archives (the Anglo-German FHS also has a set). They are:

- *Volume I: Church register copies of the eastern provinces, Posen, East & West Prussia, Pomerania and Silesia, 1994.*
- *Volume II: Archive and Church register copies of the German settlements in foreign countries: Bessarabia, Bukovina, Estonia, Lithuania, Latvia, Siebenbürgen, Sudetenland, Slovenia and South Tyrol, 1992.*
- *Volume III: Church register copies of the territories and provinces of the German Empire (with the exception of the Eastern Provinces of Prussia), 1992.*

If you discover that they hold a register of relevance to your research, you could ask them to research in it for you. However, the LDS Church has copied all of these registers and you should be able to order the microfilm through the LDS Church in the normal way (if you feel able to deal with the handwriting!). You may even find that some can be viewed on **www.familysearch.org**.

The other main source they hold is a virtually complete set of Ortssippenbücher (see pages 83–84 below) and asking them to look for you is often the quickest way to see if your ancestral parishes are covered. Though again I have heard that they have not added to their collection since 1995 and in that period many hundreds will have been published. They published a book in 1996 listing all the Ortsfamilienbücher in their collection:

- *Volume IV: Ortsfamilienbücher collected in Leipzig, by Volkmar Weiss and Katja Münchow.*

Herr Volkmar Weiss was the former head archivist of the DZfG collection and the leading spirit in keeping it going and in adding to the Ortsfamilienbuch collection. He was also of great assistance to the Anglo-German FHS when we made contact and facilitated a visit there in the 1990s. Unfortunately he lost his position there when the collection was absorbed by the Leipzig Staatsarchiv.

I have recently come across an article about the parish register portal (Kirchenbuchportal) of the Evangelical Church in Germany (**www.kirchenbuchportal.de**). They have been working on this project since 2007 and the middle phase has now been completed. You can now go online at the website (**www.kirchenbuchportal.findbuch.net**) and find for each of their parishes a full listing of the surviving records – baptisms, marriages, burials, confirmations, etc. It does not appear to be confined to the Protestant churches as Catholic dioceses and Mennonite registers are included. There are also lists of the registers for the Evangelical Church in Romania – these will cover the German-speaking area of Siebenbürgen. Access to all this information is free and the entries include the addresses of where the registers are held and how to get access to them.

The next stage will involve digitising the actual registers and putting them online. This will be expensive and we can expect that when all the registers are available online there will be a fee to access them. However, even so, imagine being able to search your ancestors' parish registers online from the comfort of your own computer! There will be no index to individual entries, at least to begin with, but it will be like reading the original registers at home. We are going to have to brush up our skills in reading the old German script!

In the meantime, I see that the parish registers for South Baden are already available to read online gratis. Go to **www.landesarchiv-bw.de/**, choose the required archive and click on "Findbuch". You can search each parish register there and download and/or print as you wish. The registers available cover 1810-70 – as do the Baden civil registers online mentioned above. I believe that they are the equivalent of Bishop's Transcripts.

Another site is: **http://matricula-online.eu**. This was a link from the Kirchenbuchportal. It covers the registers of the German Roman Catholic

Diocese of Passau. The parishes are listed in alphabetical order. There is also a useful map of the diocese enabling you to easily identify your parish and the neighbouring ones.

How I wish some British registers were as beautifully digitised and freely available online!

Wills

As in the UK, wills (Testamente or Testamentsakten) can be a fruitful genealogical source if you can only find them. They would normally have been proved in the local Amtsgerichte or Courthouse. In some cases the local family history society has indexed the local wills; for example the Bremen society, Die Maus, lists on its website (**www.die.maus-bremen.de**) wills proved in Bremen 1599-1890. Check to see what is available in your area.

The wills will be in German and handwritten so it will take some effort to find and read your ancestor's will. But it will be worth the effort.

Censuses

There were no censuses (Volkszählungen) covering the whole of the German Empire until 1871 after which censuses were taken in 1875 and every 5 years thereafter. However, the detailed schedules were destroyed after the statistics had been compiled. There were, however, many more localised ones taken by particular States for various reasons as far back as the 17th century. Where censuses were taken, as nowadays, for statistical purposes, the statistics were centralised, but the census returns, where they survive, should be in the local archives. The best course is to ask the local archives whether there are any censuses there. No doubt, as time goes by, more will be indexed or, at least, put online. Here are some examples of what is currently available.

Grand Duchy of Mecklenburg-Schwerin: There was a particularly useful census for the Grand Duchy of Mecklenburg-Schwerin in 1819: for each individual in the State it gives the name, sex, religion, date and place of birth, spouse's name and occupation, how long the individual had been living in the current parish, where and when the spouse was born and how long resident in the current parish. This census (and those for 1704 and 1751) has been indexed by the Immigrant Genealogical Society and, if you join their society, they will undertake a search and let you have the details transcribed and translated into English for a small fee (Immigrant Genealogical Society, P O Box 7369, Burbank, CA 91510-7369, USA. For their website see **feefhs.org/igs**). The census (but not the index) is available on microfilm through the LDS library. See *Mecklenburg-Schwerin Census Indexes* by Peter Towey, in the Anglo-German FHS magazine *Mitteilungsblatt*, No 47, March 1999. The LDS Church website (**www.familysearch.org**) now contains the indexed 1900 Mecklenburg-Schwerin census, part of the 1890 census which has been indexed, and the unindexed 1867 census.

Electorate of Hannover census 1852: A professional genealogist in Bremen, Regina Koppe, is gradually indexing the 1852 census for the Electorate of Hannover (much of which is now in the Land of Lower Saxony (Niedersächsen)). She has indexed and published indexes to several Counties – Amt Hoya, Amt Achim, Amt Martfeld and the town of Bodenwerder. But she has indexed much more of Hanover than that and you can search her indexes online at **www.hist.de/**. The City of Hannover itself is missing from this census but the rest seems to be complete though she has only indexed a portion of it so far. The information in the census is less detailed than English censuses, eg it does not provide the place of birth.

Heligoland (Helgoland): The island of Heligoland in the North Sea was originally Danish but became a British Colony in 1814. It was given to Germany in 1890 in exchange for Zanzibar! There are few surviving records in British archives but the Anglo-German FHS has published the census of 1881 on microfiche: *Colony of Heligoland (Helgoland). Census 5 April 1881 (CO122/37)*, Record Series Four, Anglo-German FHS, published 1999 [on 2 fiches with an index]. It is less informative than the contemporary British Census but it is complete.

Lübeck: Hansestadt Lübeck was a Free Imperial City and had separate censuses. They are online in **www.ancestry.co.uk** for 1807, 1812, 1815, 1831, 1845, 1851, 1857 & 1862 and each one is indexed. The censuses for 1871, 1875 and 1880 are on the same site but unindexed.

Schleswig-Holstein is another part of Germany that has good early census records. Schleswig and Holstein were two duchies which were part of the Holy Roman Empire and so considered, by Germans, to be German. However they belonged to the King of Denmark and were ruled from Copenhagen. Schleswig and Holstein did not become part of Prussia until 1866, after a war, as the Province of Schleswig-Holstein. After the First World War and a plebiscite, North Schleswig returned to Denmark. The censuses available mainly relate to the Danish period before 1864 and there are large parts of the census of Schleswig for 1803 online on the website of the local family history society – Arbeits-Gruppe Genealogie Schleswig-Holstein e. V. (AGGSHe.V.) (ie the Genealogy Work Group Schleswig-Holstein) **www.aggsh.de**. There is an English language version of the site but the German language version seems to contain more information – this is not uncommon so check out the German language version whenever possible. There are census transcriptions for various parishes for later censuses eg 1835, 1840 and 1860, and the whole of the census of the Fürstentum Lübeck (Principality of Lübeck) for 1819. The Principality of Lübeck had become part of the Duchy of Oldenburg in 1813 and did not include the separate city of Lübeck. I told you that the historical geography could be quite complicated!

While the German area is not so well served with censuses as Great Britain, it is worth seeing if there are such records in your area of interest.

Military and Naval Records

We often think of Germany, and particularly Prussia, as very militaristic. This is not surprising when you consider the state Prussia was left in at the end of the 17th century; having to invite new settlers to farm the depopulated lands. In the 1730s Friedrich Wilhelm I of Prussia brought in the cantonal system. The country was divided into Kreise (sometimes translated as Circles or Counties) each of which was allocated to a regiment for recruiting purposes. Each Kreis was divided into Cantons each of which was intended to provide the manpower for a Company of the Regiment. Garrisons were stationed within the cantons from which the soldiers were recruited. That system remained in force until the First World War. So if you know the place an ancestor came from you should also know which

Regiment or even Company he served in. With certain exemptions all males were expected to spend three years in initial training but stayed in the Reserve, liable to call-up, for 20 years. Volunteers to be professional soldiers could enlist for 10-12 years. The reserve undertook training with their Regiment each spring.

As they had to ensure that the Army knew who was liable to serve and when, many parishes and towns had their own lists of young men liable to military service (often prepared when the boy was baptised!) saying what happened to them; these can also serve a different function as many emigrated to avoid military service and the lists may say "nach Amerika" or "nach England".

The equivalent of the British annual "Army List" was the **"Rangliste"**. If you are interested you should be able to buy one online though they are quite expensive. The German Army Rangliste for 1906, for example, shows that the Infantry Regiment *"Duke Frederick William of Brunswick" (East Friesland) Number 78*, consisted of three companies; the first two stationed at Osnabrück and the third at Aurich. Each officer is listed and there is an overall name index of officers for the whole army. The Anglo-German FHS has copies of two German Army Ranglisten, for 1906 and 1918, which include the Württemberg Army, and the Bavarian Army Rangliste for 1918, and will make searches in them for a small fee.

First the bad news: the records of the Prussian Army, the German Army from 1871 and the records of most of the other German States' Armies after about 1867 were destroyed by fire at Potsdam in the Battle for Berlin in 1945. Virtually none of the records survived. However, those military archives that do survive are kept at the Bundesarchiv in Freiburg im Breisgau in Baden-Württemberg:

**Abt MA des Bundesarchiv,
Wiesenthalstraße 10,
D-79115 Freiburg im Breisgau,
GERMANY**

Though the main set of records do not survive, this office was responsible for keeping records of German servicemen who might be entitled to pensions or disability allowance due to war service, and so had to recreate their own records. They may well therefore have records of people who served in the German services in the 20th century. The more recent records, as in the UK, are probably closed but it is worth asking.

The German equivalent of the Commonwealth War Graves Commission, the **Volksbund Deutsche Kreigsgräberfursorge e.V**, has set up a searchable database on the Internet at **www.Volksbund.de** which would be worth searching if you think a relative may have been killed in action. The Deutsche Dienstelle, whose website is at **www.dd.wast.de**, also holds large numbers of records of German military personnel: Army and other military and paramilitary organisations for WW2, Prisoners of War, and also Naval personnel 1871-1947. Normally they will only make the information known to close relatives but it is always worth asking.

Some German States' army records, however, do survive. The **Bavarian Army** records up to 1919 are complete and are kept in the War Archive in Munich. In a very exciting move the records of individual soldiers for the First World War, 1914-18, are being placed online at **www.ancestry.co.uk**. They can be searched by name and already the details include nearly 4 million soldiers.

The records of the armies of a few other German States, like **Baden**, **Brunswick**, **Hanover**, **Hesse**, **Mecklenburg** and **Württemberg**, before 1867 (in a few cases, 1871) are kept in the individual State's archives. A useful booklet, in English, is *German Military Records as Genealogical Sources* by Horst A. Reschke, published in 1990, and available from him at PO Box 27161, Salt Lake City, UT 84127-0161, USA. This is very short, 12 pages, but lists the armies of the different States and the archives where they are kept, explains the background and gives a bibliography. The Anglo-German FHS publication, *Useful Addresses*, also contains the dates of the army records held at the various German State Archives.

It is worth noting that there were several wars involving Germans in the mid 19th century, "the Wars of Unification", as well as the Franco-Prussian War, 1870-71, which make it even more likely that your ancestor will appear in the records. To find him, though, you need to know the Army, the Regiment and the Company! As has been pointed out above, this is not necessarily as difficult as it sounds.

Particularly useful sources, where the main sets of records have been lost, are the Casualty Lists: the lists of dead, wounded and missing in each of these wars which are often published and, in many cases, available online. The casualty list for the German Army in the Franco-Prussian

War 1870-71, is on **www.ancestry.co.uk**, as are the First World War casualty lists for the German Army and the Navy, 1914-17. Each can be searched by name. Also, for the First World War, many regiments have published a commemorative history of their regiment in the war. Again these are available to purchase from second-hand book sellers online and are usually quite expensive. You will generally find, however, that each history contains lists of all the dead, wounded and missing, normally arranged by battle or campaign.

A useful source, particularly for Prussia where the other records are lost, could be the Military Church Books: each Army chaplain in the Prussian Army (and in many other German States' Armies) had his own baptism, marriage and burial registers and these often survive. There were also separate registers for each standing Garrison. These registers are only likely to record your ancestor if he married, had children baptised or was buried during his time with the army but they can be very helpful where, as with Prussia, the Army records themselves do not survive. For example Berlin Regimental church registers begin in the 1700s and the Garrison registers in 1671.

The Church books of military garrisons of the Hanoverian Army have been indexed by the late Jürgen Ritter in the series *Garnisons Hannover* covering 1690–1811 and 1816–67. The Anglo-German FHS has a set. The gap is when the Hanoverian Army was the KGL (qv) and the series ends in 1867 when the Hanoverian Army was absorbed into the Prussian Army.

The main listing of Military Church Books is *Verzeichnis der Militärkirchenbücher in der Bundesrepublik Deutschland (nach dem Stand vom 30 September 1990)* [*List of the Military Church Books in the Federal Republic of Germany (as of 30 September 1990)*] by Wolfgang Eger, published by Verlag Degener & Co, Neustadt a.d. Aisch, Germany, 1993. This volume only covers those books held in the former West Germany and about 650 volumes stored in Leipzig. The Church Books held in the rest of the former East Germany and elsewhere in the former German territories in Eastern Europe have not yet been listed, so far as I know.

For German Navy records you should try the Deutsche Dienstelle (**www.dd.wast.de**). There were Naval Churchbooks on the same lines as Army Churchbooks and these can be looked for in the same way. Where

Photograph of a soldier of the German 92nd Infantry Regiment "Braunschweig" commemorating his military service in Brunswick. Headed "Long live the Regiment that proudly calls itself the 92nd".

a German State before 1867 had its own navy, the records will probably be with the army records.

Registration of Inhabitants (Einwohnermelde)

Germany has always kept more detailed records of its inhabitants than the UK and the results, if you can get at them, can be particularly helpful for the genealogist. From about 1871 (in some places, earlier) the police kept detailed records of all residents in their district. The records were kept in the "Einwohnermeldeamt" or Residents' Registration Office. Every person was registered with details of where they came from and where they went, their family and any remarks the officials recorded. The amount of information is amazing including every address they lived at in the district covered, with the dates. As you might expect, the more recent information is usually closed, normally for 100 years, but, for periods before 1900 it is well worth tracking them down. Even for later periods it is worth trying, just in case. If not in the existing Einwohnermeldeamt for the district, the older records may well have found their way into the Stadtarchiv or Staatarchiv and I would suggest that that is where you should ask first.

Similar records are called "Melderegister". In Leipzig, for example, the Einwohnermelde-register covers 1811 to 1893 and the Melderegister covers 1890 to 1949. Both have been microfilmed by the LDS Church and are available on microfilm at the LDS libraries. You can also write (in German) to the Stadtarchiv Leipzig and ask them to extract historic information for you.

You should always check online to see what records are available. For example in **www.familysearch.org** under "Germany" you will already find vast numbers of records of individual States, cities or towns. Many of them just listed as "Miscellaneous"! When you explore them you will find inhabitants' lists as well as much else. Again they are not normally indexed though some were filmed in alphabetical order. Also **www.ancestry.co.uk**, in the card catalogue under "Germany" contains many thousands of filmed or digitised books or records which may relate to your area.

Of particular importance for immigrants to Britain who travelled via Hamburg are the Hamburg police records. They are kept at the Hamburg

Staatsarchiv but those for 1834 to 1929 have been microfilmed by the LDS Church and are available through their libraries. These records can be used to supplement the Hamburg Passenger Lists which may give the passenger's last place of residence, frequently "Hamburg", as his or her address. The police records should give his or her date and place of birth among other vital information. The same Department dealt with the issue of passports and the records from 1851 to 1929 are also available. Note that passports could be issued to people who were not citizens of Hamburg, especially if they were temporary residents who wanted to go abroad but could not get back to their home State to get a passport.

Burger Lists or Books

Another source that can enable you to place your ancestor in a specific town and time are burger lists or books. These are roughly equivalent to English Guild or Freemen's records and survive for many German cities and towns up to the mid-19th century. The books often provide useful information like occupation, address and date and place of birth. Many have been published and the LDS Library in Salt Lake City also has a large number of them. Look in the LDS Church website **www.familysearch.org** and **www.ancestry.co.uk** both of which contain quite a few.

Address Books or Directories

An "Adreßbuch" (ie Address Book), equivalent to a British trade or street directory, will often be available for most large German cities or towns from the late 18th century onwards. As in UK, the later editions often contain more detail that the earlier ones. As to availability, the most likely place to find one would be in the city or town itself but many are now online at **www.ancestry.co.uk**. They are in fact much more useful than British directories as, in many cases, the individual entries include virtually every head of household living in the town or city with their occupation. In the case of women, it will state whether they were a spinster or a wife or widow and, if a wife or widow, who her late husband was and his occupation. They are rather like an annual census – though only of heads of household. I have even found cases where they give a cross reference to an earlier address. You will find a lot of them on **www.ancestry.co.uk**.

The Berlin Adreßbücher are particularly helpful. You will find them, digitised, at the website of the Zentral & Landesbibliothek, Berlin, **adressbuch.zlb.de**. They cover the period 1799 to 1943. You can search them gratis by clicking on "Suche in den Berliner Adreßbüchern". As the entries are in alphabetical order you just need to find the right page. There is also a useful explanation in German and English explaining the order of entries eg the initial letters I and J are not distinguished and vowels with umlauts over them are listed separately after the plain vowel: ie Anton Müller comes after Zacharias Muller. They also explain the abbreviations commonly used eg "Erdg." means ground floor and "Untg." means basement.

Hamburg University has put online the address books for Hamburg and the surrounding area, including the former Danish port of Altona, at **agora.sub.uni-hamburg.de/subhh-adress/digbib/start**. These cover 1690 to 1990 and include telephone books (Fernsprechbücher) from 1881 and can be searched by name as well as browsed page by page.

Dorfsippenbücher, Ortssippenbücher and Ortsfamilienbücher

In the 1930s an organisation, the Reichssippenamt, was set up in Germany with the aim of indexing all the German parish registers and reconstituting the family trees of the families therein. By the outbreak of the Second World War only 30 parishes had been published. These were the "Dorfsippenbücher" or "village family books". The books do not just provide an index but link each individual to his or her family and the generations before and following. These were by no means the first such publications some of which date from the 19th century.

After WW2, publishing started again in the 1950s and the books were now called "Ortssippenbücher" or "Ortsfamilienbücher". Several of the volumes cover towns that are no longer, or were never, part of Germany eg the Banat now in Northern Serbia. I understand that about 200 new volumes are published each year mainly by German family history societies.

Besides the parish registers themselves, the editors of these books often made use of other archive sources in identifying and filling out the biographies of the individuals eg tax lists, emigration records, wills, censuses, etc. It is therefore always worth checking whether the town or village you are interested in has been covered by one of these Sippenbücher. Even a large City like Leipzig has been covered! Recently published Ortssippenbücher may still be available to purchase from the publishers. If you check the various family history societies' websites you will find what they have to offer.

The LDS Library in Salt Lake City and the Immigrant Genealogy Society in USA also have a large number of them. A complete listing of the extensive holdings of the Deutsche Zentralstelle für Genealogie, Leipzig, is published as *Ortsfamilienbücher mit Standort Leipzig*. The most recent edition published in 2000 lists their holdings of these books as at Autumn 1998. A further listing of the books and articles received from then to Spring 2000 was published in the magazine *Genealogie. Deutsche Zeitschrift für Familienkunde*, Heft 11/12, Band XXV, Nov-Dez 2000, pp 387-406.

The German Genealogy Computer Society (Verein für Computergenealogie) at **www.genealogy.net** has a large number of Ortssippenbücher on a database which can be searched online. There seems to be quite a lot from Lower Saxony and from Hesse which is helpful as many immigrants to UK came from there. The web address given here should take you through to the English language site. The Ortsippenbücher are shown as "local heritage books" and they can be searched individually by name. There are a surprisingly large number of such books on this site covering places that are now in Poland and other countries in Eastern Europe including Memelland – now in Lithuania. The lists are added to from time to time and I was recently astonished to find an Ortsfamilienbuch for Helgoland (Heligoland).

The former German territories in Eastern Europe

A major problem with German research that British researchers are not likely to have experienced before, is the effect of significant changes in the boundaries of the Countries concerned over the years and particularly over the last 200 years! Few countries have experienced such a number of major changes in jurisdiction and those changes are likely to have affected where the records are now to be found. This is an especial problem in the lands, east of the current German border, that had been German, or subject to the Prussian Crown, for centuries. Many of those lands are now in Poland, the Ukraine, Lithuania and even Russia (eg Kaliningrad formerly Königsberg).

There is no easy way of finding out where the records of individual cities, towns or parishes now are. It is not even easy to find out where the places are now – as so many have changed their names. The easiest way to find the place is to look in a contemporary map or atlas for the name you know and then compare it with a modern map of the area to see what it is called now. The Anglo-German FHS keeps sets of 19th and 20th century maps and offers this service to its members. Some of the name changes are relatively easy (like Danzig to Gdansk and Stettin to Szczecin) but some names have changed completely (like Bromberg to Bydgoszcz and Memel to Klaipeda). Another option is to try Googling the "old" place name but be careful to make sure that you have found the right place; as I have mentioned there were and are many places in Germany with the same or a similar name.

Once you have identified the place, you need to find out where the records are now kept. For example, many of the civil registration records for places that were in the German Empire from 1871 to 1945 but are now no longer in Germany, will still be in the town of origin. Equally, however, many were brought west by refugees at the end of each of the World Wars and are now in Standesamt I in Berlin (e-mail: **info.Stand1@labo.berlin.de**). I understand, however, that, because of staff cuts due to the current economic situation, it can take over a year to get a reply.

Many German church registers, etc. were also brought back into what is now Germany at the end of the Wars. Evangelical (Protestant) records may be in their archives in Berlin at:

Evangelisches Zentralarchiv in Berlin,
Bethaniendamm 29
D-10997 Berlin,
GERMANY
Website: www.ezab.de

Roman Catholic records may be at:

**Bischöfliches Zentralarchiv Regensburg,
St-Peters-Weg 11-13,
D-93047 Regensburg,
GERMANY
Website: www.bistum-regensburg.de.archiv**

A useful source of information on places in the former Eastern Territories is the Prussian Privy Archive in Berlin:

**Geheimes Staatsarchiv Preußicher Kulturbesitz,
Archivstraße 12-14,
D-14195 Berlin (Dahlem),
GERMANY
Website:www.gsta.spk-berlin.de**

which holds many records relating to the German population in former parts of Prussia. For example they hold the main State archives of Königsberg (now Kaliningrad, a Russian enclave on the Baltic) which had been held in the archives at Göttingen from 1953 to 1978. I understand that they are very helpful in replying to postal enquiries.

Records that have become available for research since the end of the Cold War can be very helpful in tracing people who came into Germany from the former eastern territories and the German settlements in Central, East and South East Europe, and even tracing refugees of German origin from France, Belgium, etc. during the Second World War. From 1939 to 1945 over 2.1 million people from those areas emigrated to Germany. They were required to complete pedigree charts and family group records showing documented births, marriages and deaths for each individual, their parents and their children. They were processed by the Einwandererzentralstelle (EWZ) and the indexed records generated have been microfilmed and are available at the Bundesarchiv in Berlin at:

**Abt R des Bundesarchiv,
Fickensteinallee 63,
Postfach 450 569,**

D-12175 Berlin,
GERMANY
e-mail: berlin@bundesarchiv.de

They were formerly in the Berlin Document Centre.

Also transferred from the Berlin Document Centre to the Bundesarchiv in Berlin (same address as above) were the records of the Nazi party 1933-45 which contain membership files for Nazi organisations and applications for Party membership. I understand that they are well indexed.

Another part of the Bundesarchiv holds the records relating to compensation claims by Germans displaced by the Second World War and its aftermath:

**Abt LS des Bundesarchiv,
Justus-Liebig-Straße 8A,
D-95447 Bayreuth,
GERMANY**

If the place you are interested in is now in Poland, you can start by writing to the Polish Regional Archives covering the place; you should first have ascertained where it is and its Polish name. You should write in Polish; they will reply in Polish! Now the Polish population of UK has increased so much you may well find someone locally who can help with translation – try your local Polish shop!

Parish records are much more likely to be scattered: in Poland, for example, the religion of most Poles was Roman Catholicism whereas most of the Germans there were Protestants. The Roman Catholic records are usually with the churches or the Diocese but many of the Protestant records, where they survive, may have been moved back to Germany. The Deutsche Zentralstelle für Genealogie ("German Central Office for Genealogy") in Leipzig, as mentioned above, holds large numbers of copies of the registers for the eastern provinces of Posen, East and West Prussia, Pomerania and Silesia, and for other former German-speaking territories like Bessarabia and Bukovina (in Romania), the Baltic States, Sudetenland (in the Czech Republic), Slovenia and the South Tyrol.

The LDS church has also been microfilming large numbers of registers in Eastern Europe and the microfilms can be borrowed in the usual way from FHLs or may appear on **www.familysearch.org**. A more detailed book is *A Genealogical Guide to research ancestors from East German and Sudeten German areas, from German resettlement regions in Central, Eastern and South-eastern Europe*. This was published for a German family history society, AGoFF (Arbeitgemeinschaft Ostdeutscher Familienforscher e. V.) as an English translation of their main handbook *Wegweiser*. The most recent edition of the English translation that I can find is dated 1998 but the German language version on which it was based, and thus the information in it, was dated 1995. The publisher was Verlag Degener & Co, D-91403 Neustadt a.d. Aisch, Germany, but the English language version no longer appears on their website. The book contains detailed lists of archives, homeland collections, etc. for every kreis or county in the former German Empire east of the Oder-Neisse line, and other areas of German settlement in Europe, but the most useful element for us is the historical sketch maps and potted histories of places. The Anglo-German FHS has a copy.

Advice on individual parts of Germany

Because of the many changes in names and boundaries over recent centuries, research in Germany can be confusing. Hence my advice is to get a good set of maps and to research the history of the area. There is a tendency among British researchers to presume that a Country's boundaries are permanent and that all places within those boundaries were always a part of that Country; and all those outside were not. It is not that easy on the continent. Many states were the areas ruled by an individual ruler or ruling family and they often acquired territories by marriage, war or purchase outside their original fiefdom's boundaries; rather like an English landowner might own estates in different counties. If, however, he had been a German ruler, those estates, though not physically adjacent, would often be part of his independent State. And other rulers might own parcels of land that were geographically within his territories. Much of this patchwork of statelets was sorted out by Napoleon during his rule but there were still some left in the 19th century – see eg Hesse.

One present problem is the tendency to refer to places as if the Land (ie State) they are now in is where you should look for them in the past.

The current set of Länder (States) in present-day Germany has only existed since the Second World War and for those that were in the former East Germany, only since 1990. Using those names, like Niedersächsen, Rheinland-Pfalz or Thüringen, is no help when you are researching before the Second World War, except for the overall organisation of the State archives. Even pre-WW2 States' names and boundaries often only went back to the end of WW1.

I therefore thought that these comments might be helpful to you. The German name is provided in brackets:

Alsace-Lorraine (Elsaß-Lothringen): had been French before it was conquered by Prussia in 1870 and was again from 1919. Many of the inhabitants emigrated in 1870 to avoid German rule. Many went to France but some came to UK. Those born there, who had not naturalised as British Subjects by 1914, had the shock of being interned as enemy aliens (being, in British law, legally German at the time!).

Though French is and was spoken there, many of the native inhabitants had German-looking surnames. During German rule the records were in German but the system remained that set up by the French in the 1790s and the records before 1870 and after 1918 are in French. So you benefit throughout from the great detail in the civil birth, marriage and death records.

Civil records are held in the local Mairie (Mayor's office or Town Hall) whose address you can find on the Internet. I normally e-mail (in French!) to the Mairie asking for a copy of a specific birth, marriage or death certificate. This then normally arrives by post or by e-mail, gratis, a few weeks later. I can then ask for another certificate in the same way. It might be slow but it has the advantage of not annoying the Mairie staff. If you ask for a long list of certificates in one go, they may not be so willing to provide them. This is not the place to deal with French research but there is a very different system in place and it would be worth seeing what is available on **www.ancestry.co.uk** and **www.cyndislist.com**. A French genealogical website, **www.genealogie.com**, contains indexes to large numbers of French civil registration records and covers the French Départementes that formerly made up Alsace-Lorraine: Haut Rhin, Bas Rhin, Meurthe et Moselle and Moselle. There are also French family trees to search and a forum for queries. There is a fee for joining but it does not cost a great deal.

Baden: was a Grand Duchy from 1806 and, in compensation for losing its territories in what is now France, quadrupled its territories to the east of the Rhine. Now part of the Land of Baden-Württemberg.

Bavaria (Bayern): besides the area we know as Bavaria today, the historic Kingdom included the Palatinate (Pfalz) in the west. That can be very confusing to modern researchers! Even in the German Empire, the Kingdom of Bavaria ran its own military, police, postal service and railways. It is now, minus the Palatinate, in the Land of Bavaria (Bayern).

Brunswick (Braunschweig): to quote Wendy K. Uncapher in *Lands of the German Empire and Before*, "The widely scattered pieces of Brunswick did not allow Brunswick to become a big player in German history. The constant splitting of lands among surviving sons also divided the power the ruling family once had. Tracing the multiple land divisions by family is hard enough on paper but trying to mark them on a map is utterly impossible." I think that says it all! Most of it was included within Napoleon's Kingdom of Westphalia (Westfalen). Now in the Land of Lower Saxony (Niedersächsen).

Danzig (Gdansk in Polish): was taken from Poland by Prussia in 1793 and annexed to West Prussia. It was one of the main Baltic ports. After the First World War, in 1920, Danzig was declared a Free City and it maintained that status until 1939. Much of the rest of the former Province of West Prussia became Polish as the so-called "Polish Corridor", giving Poland a sea port. After the Second World War it was incorporated in Poland as Gdansk.

Hanover (Hannover): as most English people know, the Elector of Hanover became King George I in 1714 and the Hanoverian line ruled the United Kingdom until 1837. George I (Georg Louis)'s formal title in Hanover was actually Elector of Brunswick-Lüneberg. The Electorate was overrun by France and Prussia during the Napoleonic Wars and the Hanoverian Army escaped to UK to become the King's German Legion. After the war it became a Kingdom but, because females were not allowed to succeed to the throne, when Victoria became Queen in 1837, one of her uncles, the Duke of Cumberland, became King Georg V of Hanover. Hanover took the wrong side in the Wars of Unification and was conquered by Prussia becoming a Province (Provinz Hannover) in 1866. Now in the Land of Lower Saxony (Niedersächsen).

Heligoland (Helgoland): in the North Sea opposite Hamburg, was ruled by Denmark until it was captured by the Royal Navy during the Napoleonic Wars. It was ruled as a British Colony from 1807 until 1890 when it was ceded to Germany in exchange for Zanzibar and other African territories. The inhabitants (about 2,000) were engaged in fishing and piloting ships in the North Sea. In the 1850s German recruits for the British-German Legion were registered there and then shipped to England for training. The island was evacuated and heavily bombed after the First and Second World Wars. Most surviving records are held locally: the churchbooks are at:

**Kirchenkreis Süderdithmarschen,
Kampstraße 8a,
D-25704 Meldorf,
GERMANY**

and the local civil registration records from 1875 (even though it was still a British Colony at the time) are held at:

**Gemeinde Helgoland,
Gemeinderverwaltung,
D-27498 Helgoland,
GERMANY.**

There are some records in TNA including the 1881 census for the island which has been published by the Anglo-German FHS on microfiche (though that does not give birthplaces). It has been suggested that there is a copy of the 1851 census somewhere in England too and I would be very interested if anyone can find it.

Hesse (Hessen): is very complicated. Until most of it was absorbed by Prussia in the 1860s, Hesse had consisted of a number of intertwined duchies: Electoral Hesse (Kurhessen) or Hesse-Cassel (Hessen-Kassel), which was ruled from the city of Cassel; the Grand Duchy of Hesse-Darmstadt, ruled from the city of Darmstadt; the Duchy of Nassau; the Duchy of Hesse-Homburg (ruled from Homburg); and the city of Frankfurt am Main. In the wars of unification in the 1860s Prussia defeated most of these States and created a new Prussian Province (Provinz Hessen-

Nassau) in 1867 which incorporated Electoral Hesse, Nassau, Hesse-Homburg and Frankfurt am Main. Hesse-Darmstadt survived to join the German Empire separately in 1871.

Königsberg (Kaliningrad in Russian): was Germany's major Baltic naval port and the main port of East Prussia. After the Second World War it was annexed by the Soviet Union to be their main ice-free Baltic naval port and it remained as a Russian enclave after the break-up of the Soviet Union. Not only did the Soviets expel the local population and replace them with Soviet citizens from the Soviet Union, but they renamed all the towns and villages. It was a military area closed to non-Soviet or Russian citizens until very recently. If your ancestor came from there, there is little point in visiting or attempting to research there. The administrative records of the region are now in the Prussian Privy Archives in Berlin (see page 86 above), the civil registration records should be in Standesamt I in Berlin (see page 85 above), and the church registers should be in the Church Archives in Berlin or Regensburg (see pages 85–86 above).

Mecklenburg: is on the Baltic coast and, from 1701, was divided into two duchies: Mecklenburg-Schwerin and Mecklenburg-Strelitz. The second part of the name was the capital city of each State. Both became Grand Duchies after 1815 and joined the German Empire in 1871. Now part of the Land of Mecklenburg-Vorpommern. Mecklenburg-Schwerin has a good run of searchable censuses.

Memel (Klaipeda in Lithuanian): had been part of the Province of East Prussia until the end of the First World War and the break-up of the Russian Empire. From 1923 to 1939 it was part of the independent State of Lithuania and from 1945 until the fall of the Soviet Union it was part of the Soviet Union. It has been part of the independent State of Lithuania since it achieved its freedom in 1990.

The Palatinate (Pfalz): formerly an Electorate (ie its rulers had a vote in the election of the Holy Roman Emperor) but lost out badly in the wars of the 17th and 18th century. Most of the Palatinate became part of Bavaria, the Lower Palatinate in the 1770s and much of the rest after the Napoleonic Wars. Some other parts went to Hesse and some to Baden. The former Bavarian Palatinate is now part of the Land of Rheinland-Pfalz (Rhineland-Palatinate).

Pomerania (Pommern): was formerly Swedish, and parts of it became Danish, until 1815 when it, together with the island of Rügen, became part of Prussia, called the Province of Pomerania (Provinz Pommern) from 1818. Pomerania west of the Oder River was called Western Pomerania (Vorpommern) and the part east of the Oder was Eastern Pomerania (Hinter Pommern). In 1950 the Oder-Neisse line became the dividing line between Germany and Poland so Hinter Pommern is now in Poland. The main port of Stettin, on the Oder, became Szczecin in Poland. Western Pomerania is now in the Land of Mecklenburg-Vorpommern.

Posen (Poznan in Polish): was part of Poland until the late 18th century partitions of Poland when most of it became part of Prussia (Preußen). The Prussian part, the Grand Duchy of Posen, became a Province from the 1860s. After the First World War most of it was returned to Poland as part of the Polish Corridor. It is now part of Wielkopolska (Greater Poland).

Prussia (Preußen): was by the mid-19th century by far the largest geographically, and strongest militarily, of the German States. The Kings of Prussia became Emperors of Germany when the Empire was formed in 1871. But again it is confusing as East and West Prussia were only two of the provinces of the Kingdom of Prussia. In 1919 most of West Prussia was ceded to Poland (as the Polish Corridor) effectively cutting East Prussia off from the rest of Germany. After the Second World War all of East and West Prussia became part of Poland except for the Memel (qv) region which became part of Lithuania and the major naval port of Königsberg (qv) which became the Russian enclave of Kaliningrad.

Reuss: see Thuringia.

The Rhineland: before 1815 it was made up of hundreds of tiny states and a few large ones. It was ceded to Prussia after the Napoleonic Wars and in 1824 became the Prussian Rhine Province (Rheinprovinz) often called Rhenish Prussia in English – for an amusing English view of a tour there in the late 19th century see Jerome K Jerome's *Three Men on the Bummel*. It is now divided between the lands of Nordrhein-Westfalen (North Rhine–Westphalia) and Rheinland-Pfalz (Rhineland-Palatinate).

Saarland: was part of the Prussian Rhineland from 1815 but, after WW1, was separated from Germany as a League of Nations mandate administered by France. It voted to return to Germany in a plebiscite in 1935 and has been a separate Land, the smallest, within Germany since 1957.

Saxe-Coburg-Gotha: see Thuringia

Saxony (Sächsen): is confusing because the name has been used for different Länder today, eg Lower Saxony (Niedersächsen) most of which has not been considered part of Saxony since the Middle Ages! Napoleon created a Kingdom of Saxony but it lost two fifths of its territory to Prussia at the end of the Napoleonic Wars. The capital of the Kingdom was Dresden. It is now the Land of Saxony (Sächsen). Prussia's part became the Prussian Province of Saxony (Provinz Sächsen) most of which is now in the Land of Saxony-Anhalt (Sächsen-Anhalt).

Schleswig-Holstein: was formerly two duchies called Schleswig and Holstein ruled by the King of Denmark. According to Lord Palmerston, the British Foreign Secretary: "The Schleswig-Holstein question is so complicated, only three men in Europe have ever understood it. One was Prince Albert, who is dead. The second was a German professor who became mad. I am the third and I have forgotten all about it." In any case the Question lead to war between Denmark, and Prussia, Austria and their allies. In 1866 Prussia absorbed both duchies (after war with Austria) which from 1867 formed a Prussian Province. Heligoland (Helgoland) became part of the Province in 1890 when it was acquired by the German Empire. After a plebiscite in 1920 Northern Schleswig (Nord Slesvig in Danish) was ceded to Denmark. Many inhabitants of the duchies who did not want to be ruled by Prussia emigrated to UK and elsewhere in the mid-19th century. It is now part of the Land of Schleswig-Holstein.

Silesia (Schlesien): was the subject of various wars between Prussia and Austria in the 18th century but Prussia ended up with most of it. It became the Prussian Province of Silesia (Provinz Schlesien) in 1815 and remained so until after the First World War. After the Second World War it became part of Poland except for a few counties (Kreise) west of the Neisse River which eventually became part of the Land of Saxony.

Thuringia (Thüringen): for most of the last 500 years was divided into various "Saxon Duchies". When the German Empire was created in 1871 they joined as: the Grand Duchy of Sachsen-Weimar-Eisenach; the Duchies of Sachsen-Meiningen, Sachsen-Coburg-Gotha and Sachsen-Altenburg; the Principalities of Schwarzburg-Rudolstadt, Schwarzburg-Sonderburg and Reuss (Alterer und Jungere Linien) (ie older and younger branches of the family). In English the "Sachsen" element of the names was normally replaced by "Saxe" as in Saxe-Coburg-Gotha,

Prince Albert's homeland. These are all now in the Land called Thuringia (Thüringen).

The House of **Reuss** practices an unusual system of naming and numbering the male members of the family, every one of which for centuries has borne the name "Heinrich". While most royal and noble houses give numbers only to the reigning head of the house, and that in the order of their reign, the Reuss Younger Line used a numbering sequence for all male family members which began and ended roughly as centuries began and ended. In consequence of this naming system, certain heads of the Reuss Younger Line have had the highest numbers attached to their name of any European nobility. Note also that the male children within a single nuclear family need not bear sequential numbers, as all members of the larger family use a common numbering system. For example, the sons of Prince Heinrich LXVII Reuss of Schleiz, in order of their births, used the names Heinrich V, Heinrich VIII, Heinrich XI, Heinrich XIV, and Heinrich XVI.

Westphalia (Westfalen): is also very complicated! Napoleon, in 1807, created a Kingdom of Westphalia out of parts of many different States. After the Napoleonic Wars it was dissolved though most went to Prussia and became the Province of Westphalia (Provinz Westfalen). It is now part of the Land of Nordrhein-Westfalen (North Rhine-Westphalia).

Kingdom of Württemberg: like Baden, the Kingdom of Württemberg did well out of the Napoleonic Wars, losing its territories in what is now France, but gaining much territory to the east of the Rhine. Now part of the Land of Baden-Württemberg.

To illustrate the possibilities of finding useful records in different States, there are the **Familienregistern** (Family Registers) of the Kingdom of Württemberg (within its 1806 borders). The registers were the result of a Government decree of 1806 but were actually kept by the parish priest. Each family has a separate page or pages and entries contain the name of the head of household, his date & place of birth (ie not baptism though that might also be included), social standing, profession, residence, date & place of marriage and of death; similar details for the spouse, his and her parents and his children. All entries are cross-referenced to other families in the parish where necessary. All registers are fully indexed and all parishes are covered from 1815 onwards (so, as people alive in 1806 were covered, the entries could go back to the mid 18th century!).

Unfortunately the German privacy laws mean that the information after 1900 may not be available (but it is worth asking!). The LDS Church has microfilmed nearly all of the records and these are listed under "church records" in their Catalog and so can be ordered in the usual way. The original records are usually still in the parish with the churchbooks. The main problem in reading them is that they are in the old script and the handwriting is often small and scribbled!

States outside the German Empire with significant German-speaking Populations

The Austro-Hungarian Empire

Many lands that had significant German-speaking populations were formerly part of the Austro-Hungarian Empire: the Czech Republic, Slovakia, Hungary, the Italian Tyrol, Romania, and Serbia and most of the other successor states of Yugoslavia. The problems and solutions are much the same as for the former German Eastern Provinces.

In the Austrian Empire (it was not renamed the Austro-Hungarian Empire until 1867 when the Kingdom of Hungary was granted Home Rule under the Austrian Crown) there was no civil registration as such. Up to 1781, the local Roman Catholic priest was expected to include in his parish registers details of everyone in the parish whatever their religion: whether Catholic, Protestant, Jewish, Muslim or of no religion. If you are lucky there may also survive a parish "Status Animarum" ("Condition of the Souls") which lists everyone in the parish with details of their family, religion, morals, etc. The Jewish community was allowed to keep its own records after 1781 but Protestants not until 1849. Civil registration in Austria itself started as late as 1939.

Austria
Try **http://matricula-online.eu**. If you have Austrian ancestors this is for you! When you get to the website translate it into English by clicking on the Union Jack. You will find Austrian and German collections. The Austrian section includes the **Roman Catholic Diocese of St Pölten** and lists all the parishes in alphabetical order. When you find your parish you

can access the original registers in excellent quality digital images. You can adjust the size and the contrast if necessary. I have not checked all of the registers but some seem to be in the German language and in old German script though the earlier ones will be in Latin. A bonus is that many go up to 1939! Civil registration in Austria did not start until 1939.

There are also the registers in the State Archives of **Upper Austria** (Oberösterreicher Landesarchiv). Again they are in alphabetical order and I noticed that the lists included several indexes including eg Abtsdorf death index 1690-2006! The Roman Catholic Archdiocese of **Vienna (Wien)** is also there and has an alphabetical list of parishes whose records you can see. Unfortunately for the City of Vienna itself it only lists one parish: "Unsere Liebe Frau zu den Schotten" (Our Lady of the Scots) though it does include registers relating to Maria am Gestade, Spital in der Rossau and St Rosalia. Possibly their records were kept with the main parish's records. There are a very large number of parishes covered in the Archdiocese's records and many of them are probably suburbs of Vienna today. The Matricula site claims that more parishes will be added as many are already digitised. So it would repay a visit from time to time.

While in the same site, go to the "Tools" drop down menu and click on "Resources". You will find that the Austrian **Voralberger** Landesarchiv has a separate site listing and providing free access to the registers in their keeping. They say that these are taken from microfilm but the pictures look just as good to me!

As an example of some other records that might survive, let us take the City of **Vienna (Wien)**. Useful sources are: "Einwohnermeldezettel" (population register cards) 1850-1920 which are arranged alphabetically with males first followed by females; Einwohnerkartei (population registers) 1700-1950 also arranged alphabetically; indexes to Vienna wills (Testamente) 1548-1850 and estates (Verlaßenschaften) 1789-1850; passport registers (Paßregister) 1792-1918; workers' registers (Arbeiterprotokolle) 1860-1919, and Nazi pedigree documentation (Abstammungsnachweise) 1938-45, all of which are indexed. There are also military personnel files (Grundbuchblätter) 1780-1930 for soldiers born in the City of Vienna, arranged alphabetically.

Incidentally those **military personnel files** should survive for all the former parts of the Austro-Hungarian Empire. They were held alphabetically by province and those relating to former provinces that are no longer part of Austria should have been sent to the archives of the successor states eg those for Hungary should be in Budapest. The difficulty arises when the former province has been split between Countries. It is best to start by writing to the War Archives in Vienna at:

**Osterreichisches Staatsarchiv,
Kreigsarchiv,
Nottendorfergasse 2,
A-1030 Wien,
AUSTRIA**

All the above records for Vienna, and many others, have been microfilmed by the LDS church and should be available through their local Libraries.

The Czech Republic
At **http://matricula-online.eu** there are also separate links to three Czech websites: the Moravian Provincial Archives at Brno, the Opava Regional Archives (covering parishes in Northern Moravia) and the State Regional Archives in Trebon, covering part of Bohemia. Each seems to deal with the registers in slightly different ways and I noticed in Trebon that they have digitised a large number of other records including three censuses between 1857 and 1880.

A useful blog on Czech genealogy is at **czechgenealogy.blogspot.co.uk** and lists other Czech archives which have registers online.

Hungary
In Hungary, civil registration started on 1st October 1895 and the records are kept in the local town halls though the National Archives has duplicates and will undertake a search for you. You should write, in Hungarian, German or English to:

**Magyar Orszagos Leveltar,
Becsikapu ter 4, Postafiok 3,
H-1250 Budapest 1,
HUNGARY**

Hungary is much smaller now than it was from 1895 to 1919 and many of the former Hungarian areas are now in surrounding countries like Slovenia, Croatia, Serbia (especially the Vojvoidina), the Czech Republic, Slovakia, Romania and the Ukraine. On the other hand, the archives of the Austro-Hungarian State before 1919 are likely to be useful for records such as censuses and Army and Navy records. To do research in the area of the Austro-Hungarian Empire during the last 100 years or so, you really need a good history of the area and a good set of maps!

Denmark

The present German Land of Schleswig-Holstein was ruled by the King of Denmark until it was conquered by Prussia in 1864. Germany also included North Schleswig from 1864 until it was returned to Denmark in 1920. Altona, which is now a central suburb of Hamburg, was a Danish port until 1864! If your researches take you back to this area before the 1860s, you will need to use the Danish archives some of which are held locally but some are in Copenhagen. Civil registration in Denmark did not start until 1874 but the church records are good and should still be held locally as in Germany. Surnames can be a problem as the patronymic system (being named after the father without a true surname eg Pedersen) often continued in rural areas until the mid 19th century.

Online there are large numbers of searchable databases, eg the Royal Danish Archives website, arkivalieronline.dk (**www.sa.dk/ao/English/**) provides access to the digitised parish registers up to 1892 (and sometimes very much later) and to Danish censuses from 1787 to 1930. The Danish Emigration Archives 1869-1940 are at **www.emiarch.dk**.

For more basic advice on research in Denmark see the LDS "Denmark" webpage available under "Learn" on **www.familysearch.org**, and *Genealogical Guidebook & Atlas of Denmark*, by Frank Smith & Finn A Thomsen, Thomsen's Genealogical Centre, P O Box 588, Bountiful, Utah 84010, USA, 4th edition, 1998. The latter contains useful maps of the administrative areas of Denmark at different times and a gazetteer of parishes and other places. The Anglo-German FHS has a copy.

The Russian Empire

In the Russian Empire pre-1917 many of the official and merchant classes in the Baltic area were people of German descent: Baltic Germans. They had German names, often intermarried and continued to speak German even though their families had lived there from before the Reformation. Most of them were Lutherans unlike their Russian neighbours who were Russian Orthodox by religion. After the First World War and the break-up of the Russian Empire three new States emerged along the Baltic Coast: **Lithuania**, **Latvia** and **Estonia**. After the Second World War they were incorporated into the Soviet Union but regained their independence when the Soviet Union broke up. The LDS Church website, **www.familysearch.org**, under "Search" has a useful introduction called "Baltic Genealogical Profile" which outlines the records available in each Country and how to access them.

The **Latvian Archives** are particularly helpful as there is now a website where you can access the country's church registers gratis: **www.lvva.raduraksti.lv/** ("Raduraksti" means "Genealogy"). The homepage should be in English but, if not, click on "EN" in the top right. You need to register which is quick and easy. You then have access, amongst other records, to the parish registers. There are no indexes so far as I can see but you can search through the church books page by page as you would with the register itself. The Lutheran registers are in the old German script.

Similarly for **Estonia** you can search the parish registers online. Go to **www.eha.ee/english.english.htm** which takes you through to the Estonian Historical Archives (Ajalooarhiiv). Again you need to register which is also quick and easy. Then click on Saaga which takes you through to the digitised archival sources. The registers are in alphabetical order. Again there are no indexes but good-quality digitised pictures of each page.

I have not found anything similar for **Lithuania** but the archives are online at **www.archyvai.lt**. You can write to them in English for help but must provide the name, town and religion of the ancestor you are researching.

The best way to research in **Russia** is via **BLITZ – USA, 907 Mission Avenue, San Rafael, California, 94901 – 2910, USA**. You can write in English and pay in US dollars. I have used this service several times in the past to do research in Moscow or St Petersburg (formerly Leningrad) and found them very helpful and the charges reasonable. Once you have made contact via USA you are given the e-mail address of the researcher in the archives in St Petersburg to deal with. I have found that the researcher has reasonable English and is helpful.

Poland

Poland is a very special case. It ceased to exist as an independent country in 1793 having been partitioned between the Prussian, Russian and Austrian Empires. Despite some of the Russian share being called "Congress Poland", after the Congress of Vienna settled the state of Europe after the Napoleonic Wars, it was still part of the Russian Empire. The "Grand Duchy of Warsaw" was a short-lived quasi-independent state, ruled by the King of Saxony, for a few years under the Napoleonic occupation.

The Russian part of Poland often appears in British records of immigrants as "Russian Poland". Within the Russian Empire Jews were only allowed to live within the Pale of Settlement much of which was in Russian Poland. If the immigrant came from the Prussian part, they would be listed as from Prussia or Germany.

The parts of the former independent Poland that became part of Prussia included Posen, parts of Silesia and large parts of East and West Prussia. As mentioned under "Prussia" above, most of these gains went to the newly independent state of Poland after the First World War and the rest after the Second World War. The Austrian share of pre-1793 Poland was relatively small but that also went to Poland in the 20th century.

The redrawing of the boundaries of Poland after the Second World War was drastic with many areas that had been Polish between the wars, becoming part of the states of Belarus and Ukraine. The areas from which German-speaking emigrants usually left in the last few centuries were mainly in the Prussian share, or the western part of the Austrian share, so should now be in Poland.

To do research in the former parts of Germany or Austria that are now part of Poland, you will need to find out where the relevant records now are. For advice on how to do that, see the section on the former German territories in Eastern Europe, above.

Switzerland

Swiss citizens gain their citizenship from their family's home town or village and, even if an individual has moved away, their birth, marriage and death details are still sent back to the home town and recorded there – even from another Country. You therefore need to know the family's home town or village. Civil registration did not start until 1st January 1876 but the parish registers can go back to the 16th century and are often found in the same office. In many cases full genealogies have been compiled by the local authorities – some of which employ a full-time genealogist!

Abbreviations

AGFHS = The Anglo-German Family History Society

AGGSH = Schleswig-Holstein Genealogy Workgroup (Arbeits-Gruppe Genealogie Schleswig-Holstein e.V).

AGoFF = East Germany FHS (Arbeitsgemeinschaft Ostdeutscher Familienforscher e. V.)

ASTAKA = German genealogical index at Leipzig (Ahnenstammkartei)

CWGC = Commonwealth War Graves Commission

EWZ = German Immigration records of WW2 (Einwandererzentralstelle, Berlin)

FEEFHS = Federation of Eastern European Family History Societies

FHS = Family History Society

FHL = Family History Library

ICRC = International Committee of the Red Cross, Geneva

JGSGB = Jewish Genealogical Society of Great Britain

KGL = King's German Legion

LDS Church. The Church of Jesus Christ of Latter-Day Saints; sometimes called the Mormons

POW = Prisoner of War

TNA = The National Archives at Kew; formerly the Public Record Office

UK = United Kingdom

USSR = Union of Soviet Socialist Republics; Soviet Union

WW1 = First World War

WW2 = Second World War

Index

1848 refugees 10
60th Regt of Foot 28

A

Abstdorf, Upper Austria, death
 indexes 1690-2006 97
address books (Adreßbücher) – see
 under German – Directories
Adelslexikon 52
adresbuch.zlb.de 83
Ahnenstammkartei (ASTAKA) 71
Aldershot, Hampshire 30
Alexandra Palace, London 46
aliens, records of 8, 17-18, 37
"Almanac de Gotha" 52
Altona – see Denmark, censuses, &
 Hamburg
Alsace-Lorraine
 (Elsaß-Lothringen) 63, 89
 French Départementes 89
American War of Independence 10, 28
Amtsgericht (District court) 69, 74
Anglo-German Family History
 Society (AGFHS) 8, 85, 99
 Name Index 8, 18-27, 37-38
 publications 8, 18, 25, 30, 38-39
  41, 43, 46, 91
 Research Guides 18, 58, 65
 Tracing Your German Ancestors 65
 Useful Addresses 70, 78
Anhalt – see Saxony
anti-German hysteria 44
Antwerp, Belgium 57
Appelsee in Livland 53
SS "Arandora Star" 47
Arbeitsgemeinschaft Ostdeutscher
 Familienforscher e. V. (AGoFF) 88
Archives:
 Austria 96-98

Denmark 99
Germany 70-83
 Addresses 77
 army list, German (Ranglisten) 77
 army records 76-81
  Austrian 97-98
  – See also Vienna
  Baden 78
  Bavarian 77, 78
  British 10, 28-32, 43
  Brunswick 78
  German Empire 76-81
  Hanover 30, 78, 79
  Hesse 78
  Mecklenburg 78
  Prussian 76-77
  Württemberg 77-78
artists 43
Augsburg 23
Aurich 77
Austria 59, 93-94, 96-98, 101
 civil registration 96
 – see also Abstdorf
 – see also St Pölten
 – see also Upper Austria
 – see also Voralberg
Austro-Hungarian Empire 96-99
 army records 97, 98
 civil registration 96
Auswanderer or German Emigrant
 records 54-55

B

Bach, Johann Christian 43
Baden, Grand Duchy of 21, 55, 63
  69, 90, 92
 archives at Freiburg im Breisgau
  69, 77
 army records 78

104

churchbooks online 73
Baden-Württemberg 69, 95
   archives at Ludwigsburg 55
bakers 41
Baltic States – see also Estonia, Latvia
   & Lithuania 87, 99-100
Banat, The, Serbia 83
banking 35, 68
baptism registers – see churchbooks
Bas Rhin – see Alsace-Lorraine
Barings Bank 35
Bavaria (Bayern) 90, 92
   army records 78
Bavarian Embassy RC Chapel,
   London 22
Begräbnisse – see Churchbooks
Belarus 101
Berechurch, Camp 186, Essex 48
Berlin 65
   Adreßbücher 1799-1943 83
   Berlin Document Centre 86-87
   Bundesarchiv 77, 86-87
   Evangelical Central Archives 85
   Garrison churchbooks 79
   Prussian Privy Archives 86
   Regimental churchbooks 79
   Standesamt I 85
Bernard, Roy & Margaret 8
Bessarabia (Bessarabien) 87
Bessarabien – see Bessarabia
Bexhill, Sussex 30
Blackheath, London 35-37
BLITZ – USA 100
Bohemian archives, Trebon 98
Bovenizer 37
Bradford, Yorkshire, German church 24
Braunschweig – see Brunswick
Bremen, 35, 39, 63
   Bremen Family History Society
      "Die Maus" 56
   Bremen-Verden, Duchy of 39

passenger lists 56
– see also wills
Bremerhaven 56
   passenger lists 56
Brighton German church 24
British Armed Services, records 28-32
   1861 British Army census 31
British-German Legion 30-31, 91
British Library, Indian records 31, 34-35
Brno archives – see Czech Republic
Bromberg (Bydgoszcz) 85
Brunswick (Braunschweig), Duchy of 55, 90
   army records 78
   Brunswick 92nd Infantry
      Regiment "Braunschweig" 80
Brunswick-Lüneburg – see Hanover
Bukovina (Bukowina) 87
Bulgaria 44
Bürgerlich families 52-53
Burger lists or books 82
burial registers – see churchbooks
Bydgoszcz – see Bromberg

C

C. A. Starke Verlag, Limburg a/L,
   genealogical publishers 53
Camberwell German Evangelical
   Church, London 23
canton 76
Cape Colony Police 31
Carl Rosa Opera Company 43
Cassel – see Hesse
censuses 11-12, 74-76
   British censuses 11, 12, 31
   Danish censuses 1787-1930, 99
      digitised online (www.sa.dk/
      ao/English/) 99
   German censuses 74-76
      Hanover 1852 75

Heligoland 1851 & 1881 75
Lübeck, Free City, 1807, 1812,
    1815, 1831, 1845, 1851,
    1857 & 1862 75
Lübeck, Principality 1819 75
Mecklenburg-Schwerin &
    Mecklenburg-Strelitz 74-75
Schleswig 1803 76
Central register of Aliens 18
Chapel Royal – see St James Palace
charities, German in London 25-26
Chelsea Hospital 31
Christchurch, Kensington
    (Christuskirche) 18, 22
churchbooks (Kirchenbücher) 70-74
    baptism register (Taufregister) 70
    burial register (Begräbnisse) 71
    confirmation register
        (Konfirmation) 70
    death register (Sterberegister) 71
    marriage register (Trauregister) 70
    military 79
    naval 79
    regimental 79
"Church Books: Beyond the Basics,
    German" 70
circle (Kreis) 76
Colchester, Essex 30-31
Commonwealth War Graves
    Commission (CWGC) 32
Computergenealogie, Verein für
    (German Computer Genealogy
    Society) 58-59, 84
Confederation of the Rhine 60
confirmation registers – see
    churchbooks
Congress Poland 101
Coniston 23
Cornwall 23
county – see circle
Cresswell, Yvonne 45-46
Crew List Index Project (CLIP) 34

Crimean War 39
Croatia 98
Cumbria 93
Cyndi's List Website 58, 89
Czechoslovakia 87, 98
Czech Republic 87, 98
    – Bohemian archives, Trebon 98
    – Czech genealogy blog
        (czechgenealogy.blogspot.
        co.uk) 98
    – Moravian archives, Brno &
        Opava 98

D

Danzig (Gdansk) 56, 85, 90
Darmstadt – see Hesse
Davis, Gwen – see King's German
    Legion
death registers – see churchbooks
denization records 12-17
Denmark 75-76, 99
    Altona 83, 99
    Archives, Royal Danish
        (**arkivalieronline.dk**) 99
    civil registration 99
    censuses 75-76
    emigration archives 1869-1940
        (**www.emiarch.dk**) 99
    family history research 99
    parish registers, digitized to 1892
        (**www.sa.dk/ao/English/**) 99
    patronymic naming system 99
    – See also Heligoland
    – See also Schleswig-Holstein
Deutsche Dienststelle 48, 78
Deutsches Geschlechterbuch 52-53
Deutsche Zentralstelle für Genealogie
    (DZfG) 71-73, 84, 87
Dietrich Bonhoeffer Church – see
    Sydenham German Evangelical
    Church

directories – see under German
"Discovery", TNA Online catalogue
      12-17, 32, 33, 47
Dolmage   37
Dorfsippenbücher (Village Family
 Books)   83-84
 – see also Ortssippenbücher &
  Ortsfamilienbücher
Douglas Camp – see Isle of Man
Dover   37
Dublin German Church 18, 24-25

E

Eastcote POW Camp 46
Eastern Europe   84-88
East India Company 10, 34-35
East Prussia (Ostpreußen) 87-88, 92-93
Elbe-Weser Dreieck 40
Eden, Camp 83, Malton, North
 Yorkshire   48
Edinburgh German Church 24
Einwandererzentralstelle (EWZ),
 Berlin   86-87
Einwohnermeldeamt – see Residents'
 Registration Office
Einwohnermelde – see Residents'
 Registers
Elector, (Kurfürst)   51
Elsaß-Lothringen – see Alsace-
 Lorraine
Embassy Chapels, London 22
Embury   37
emigrants – see Auswanderer
 – see also Denmark
English Heritage   48
Estland – see Estonia
Estonia (Estland) 53, 100
Evangelical Central Archive, Berlin
 (Evangelisches Zentralarchiv)85, 92

F

Families in Bristiah India Society
 (FIBIS)   34-35
Family Search 62, 72, 75, 81-82,
     87-88, 99, 100
farm surnames   50
Federation of Eastern European
 Family History Societies
 (FEEFHS)   75
Fernsprechbücher – see Telephone
 Books and under Hamburg
Find My Past   34
First World War 11, 32-33
 German casualty lists 1914-17 79
Folkestone, Kent   37
France,   93, 95
 Civil Registration 89
 Historical Geography 89
 – see also Napoleonic Wars
Franco-Prussian War, 1870-1871, 78
 German Casualty Lists 78-79
Frankfurt am Main   92
Freedom of Information Act 17
Freeman, Pam 8, 18, 19
Freiburg im Breisgau – see Baden
Freiherr (Baron)   52
Fulham, St Mark's German Church 18,
       22
Fürst (Prince)   51

G

Gdansk – see Danzig
Genfair – **www.genfair.com** 8
Genealogisches Handbuch des Adels 52
German
 alphabet   62-64
 bands   43
 censuses   74-76
 Central Office for Genealogy,
  Leipzig (Deutsche

Zentralstelle für Genealogie) 71-73
churches in UK 18-25
church registers 8, 18-25, 70-74
church schools in London 25
civil registration 63-69
coats of arms (Wappen) 53-54
directories (Adreßbücher) 82-83
Eastern Europe, former German
   Territories in 63
emigration museums 56
family history societies 58, 83
inhabitants' registers
   (Einwohnermelde) 81-82
gazetteer – see "Meyer's Orts-
   und Verkehrs-Lexikon des
   Deutsches Reichs"
genealogical dictionaries 51-53
historical geography 12, 59-62, 88-89
Lands of present day 61
mercenaries 28
merchant seamen 24
military and naval records 48, 76-81
miners 23
names 49-50
   – see also farm surnames
nobility 51-53
   – see also C. A. Starke Verlag
   & Starke Index of German
   Nobility
occupations in UK 38-43
online sources 58-59, 62, 69
records microfilmed by the LDS
   Church 62
refugees in ww2 86-87
regiments in British Army 28-29
"Research Companion, The
   German" 58
scripts 37, 62-64
telephone directories 50-51
titles 51-52

War Graves Commission
   (Volksbund Deutsche
   Kriegsgräberfursorge e. V.)78
Germany 10, 12
Gibbons, Sue 41
Glasgow 24
Gorey, Co. Wexford 25
"Gothaischen Genealogischen
   Hofkalendar" 52
Göttingen archives 86
Goulston Street German Church –
   see St Paul's German Reformed
   Church, London
Graf (Count or Earl) 52
Großherzog (Grand Duke) 51
Grote, Andreas (1710-86) 35
Grundbuchblätter – see Military
   Personnel files

H

hairdressers 41, 43
Hallé Orchestra 43
Hamburg 39, 65, 99
   Adreßbücher 1690-1990 83
   passenger lists 56, 62
   police records 81-82
   telephone books from 1881 83
Hamburg Lutheran Church, London19
Händel, George Frederick 43
Hanover (Hannover) 10, 30, 50, 63, 90
   census 1852 75
   Government in London 38
   – see also King's German Legion
Harperley POW Camp, Camp 93,
   County Durham 48
Haut Rhin – see Alsace-Lorraine
Heligoland (Helgoland) 84, 90-91, 94
   censuses 1881 & 1851 75
   records 84, 91
   – see also British-German Legion

Hellen, Dr J Anthony 47-48
Herschell, Friedrich Wilhelm 43
Herzog (Duke) 52
Hesse (Hessen) 84, 88, 91-92
   army records 78
   Electoral Hesse (Kurhessen) 91-92
   Hesse-Cassel (Hessen-Kassel) 91-92
   Hesse-Darmstadt (Hessen-Darmstadt) 91-92
   Hesse-Homburg (Hessen-Homburg) 91-92
   Hessen-Nassau 91-92
   Nassau 91-92
Hessian mercenaries 10, 28
Hinter Pommern – see Pomerania
Historic Chapels Trust 20
Hofnamen – see farm surnames
Holbein, Hans 43
Holstein – see Schleswig-Holstein
Holy Roman Empire 54, 60
Homburg – see Hesse
Home Office 12, 16-17
Hooper Square, German Church, – see St Paul's German Reformed Church, London
Hospital, The German, Dalston, London 39, 41, 42
Huguenot Society 14-15
Hull German Church 24
Hungary 97, 98-99
   civil registration 98-99
   – duplicates in National Archives 98
   – National Archives 98
   – see also Austro-Hungarian Empire
Huyton Camp 48

I

immigration records 11
   The Palatines of 1709 35-37
   ships' passenger lists and aliens certificates 37-38
   indexes – see AGFHS Name Index
India 34-35
   Indian Mutiny 31, 34
Infantry Regiment "Duke Frederick William of Brunswick" (East Friesland) Nr 78 77
International Committee of the Red Cross, Geneva (ICRC) 44-45
International Lutheran Students' Centre, Sandwich Street 19
Internment 44-48
   First World War 11, 44-46
      Camps 44-46
   Second World War 46-48
      Camps 46-48
      Tribunals 47
Ipswich, Suffolk 30
Ireland, 14-17, 35-37
   Northern Ireland 16, 24-25
   German Church, Dublin 24-25
   Republic, of 16, 24-25
Isle of Man 44-48
   Douglas Camp 44-48
   Knockaloe Camp 44-48
   Manx National Heritage museum 45-46
Islington German Lutheran Church, London 23

J

Jerome, Jerome K 93
Jewish Genealogical Society of Great Britain (JGSGB) 27
Jewish records 17-18, 27-28, 96
   Plymouth Aliens List 17-18
Jones, Henry Z. 36

K

Kaiserswerth Institute, Deaconesses – see Hospital, German
Kaliningrad – see Königsberg
Kassel – see Hesse
Kaufmann, Angelika 43
Keswick 23
Kew, St Anne 43
Kilmainham Hospital 31
King George I 10, 38
King George III 10
King's German Legion 8, 10, 29-30, 90
Kirchenbuch – see Churchbooks
Kirchenbuchportal (**www.kirchenbuchportal.de**) 73
Klaipeda – see Memel
Kneller, Sir Godfrey 43
Knockaloe Camp – see Isle of Man
Koblenz, German Archives 45
Konfirmation – see churchbooks
König (King) 52
Königsberg (Kaliningrad) 56, 85, 86, 92, 93
Kreis – see circle
Kurfürst (Elector) 51
Kurhessen – see Hesse

L

Ladies' Clothing Society of St George, Alie Street 25-26
LDS Church – see also Family Search 62, 71
   libraries in UK 62, 82
   Salt Lake City Library 84
   online catalog 62, 87-88
Landesarchiv (State [Land] archives) 69
Langdon Hills, Camp 266, Essex 48
Latvia (Lettland) 100
Le Havre, France 57
Leipzig 71-73, 79, 84
   Einwohnermelde 1811-93 81

Melderegister 1890-1949 81
Lettland – see Latvia
Lippe-Detmold 50
Litauen – see Lithuania
Lithuania (Litauen) 84, 85, 92, 93, 100
Liverpool German Church 24
London, 10-11
London, City of 35
   freedom records 35
   Livery Companies' records 35
London, East End of 10
London, German Churches in 18-23
London Livery Companies 35
London Metropolitan Archives 34, 35
Lower Saxony (Niedersächsen) 55, 84, 90, 93
Lübeck, Free City, (Hansestadt Lübeck) 75-76
   censuses 75-76
Lübeck, Principality of, (Fürstentum Lübeck) 76
   censuses 75-76
SS "Lusitania" 44
Lutherhaus – German girls' home in London 27

M

Manchester German Church 24
Marks, Graham 46
marriage registers – see churchbooks
Matricula website (**matricula-online.eu**) 73-74, 96-97, 98
Mawer, Brian 38-39
Mecklenburg-Schwerin & Mecklenburg-Strelitz 74-75, 92
   army records 78
   – see also German censuses
Mecklenburg – Western Pomerania (Mecklenburg-Vorpommern) 92
medals, military, British campaign 33
Memel (Klaipeda) 85, 92, 93

Memelland 84
Mendelssohn, Felix 43
Mennonite 73
Merchant Navy 24, 33-34, 43
Metropolitan Police 18
Metzner, Len, indexes – see also
 AGFHS Name Index 8, 19, 30, 31, 37-38
Meurthe et Moselle – see Alsace-Lorraine
"Meyer's Orts- und Verkehrs-Lexikon des Deutsches Reichs" 60, 65
MI5 12
military churchbooks 79
military personnel files, Austro-Hungarian Empire (Grundbuchblätter) 97-98
 – see also Vienna
militia 31
miners 23
Mitteilungsblatt – AGFHS quarterly journal 8, 21, 75
Moravian archives, Brno 98
 – see also Matricula website
 – see also Northern Moravia archives
Mormons – see LDS Church
Moselle – see Alsace-Lorraine
musicians 43
 Musikantentum Museum, Bad Lichtenberg 43
Müthel – see v. Müthel family

N

Napoleonic Wars 10, 29-30, 32-33, 63, 91, 92, 93, 95, 101
Nassau – see Hesse
National Archives, the (TNA) – see also "Discovery" 12, 14, 28, 32-34, 37-38, 44-48, 91
national service in Germany 76-77
naturalisation records 12-17, 34

navy, records 79, 81
Nazi Party records 1933-45 87
 – see also Vienna
New York 35-37
Newcastle upon Tyne German Church 24
Niedersächsen – see Lower Saxony
Nightingale, Florence 39
Nordrhein-Westfalen – see North Rhine-Westphalia
North German Confederation 60
North Rhine-Westphalia (Nordrhein-Westfalen) 93, 95
Northern Moravia archives, Opava 98
 – see also Matricula website
Noschke, Richard 46

O

Oder-Neiße line 93
Oldenburg, Duchy of 50, 63
Opava archives – see Czech Republic
orphanage, German, in London 27
Ortssippenbücher & Ortsfamilienbücher (Village Family Books) 72, 83-84
 – see also Dorfsippenbücher
Osnabrück 77
Osterholz bei Hemelingen, Bremen 60, 62
Osterholz-Scharmbeck 60

P

Palatinate, The (Pfalz) 21, 35-37, 43, 63, 92
 Bavarian Palatinate – see Bavaria
Palatines of 1709, the 25, 35-37
Pale of Settlement in Russian Empire 101
Panayi, Prof Panikos 44
Parliamentary Archives 16
Passau, Roman Catholic Diocese of 73-74

111

passenger lists 37-38, 56-57, 62
Peninsular War, The 30
Phoenix Insurance Company 39
plebiscite 76, 93, 94
Plymouth, Devon 17
Poland 57, 84, 85, 93, 94, 101
   archives 87
Polish Corridor 93
Pomerania (Pommern) 87, 92-93
   – see also Mecklenburg
Pommern – see Pomerania
poorhouse, German, in London 25
pork butchers 41
Posen (Posznan) 87, 93, 101
Postal History Society 46
postcodes, German 63-64
Price, Amanda 25
Prince Albert 94
Prisoner of War Information Bureau,
   Covent Garden 45-46
POW Camps in WW1 44-46
POW Camps in WW2 46-48
   Camp 83, Eden, Essex 48
   Camp 93, Harperley, Co Durham 48
   Camp 186, Berechurch, Essex 48
   Camp 266, Langdon Hills, Essex 48
   Huyton Camp, 48
Prussia (Preußen) 63, 87, 92, 93, 101
   military organisation 76-77
Prussian Embassy Protestant Chapel,
   London 22
Prussian Privy Archives (Geheimes
   Staatsarchiv Preußischer
   Kulturbesitz) 86, 92
Preußen – see Prussia
Public Records Office, Dublin 16

Q

Queen Victoria 90

R

Rangliste – see Army List
Rathaus (Town Hall) 63
Rathkeale, Co. Limerick 25
Regensburg – see under Roman
   Catholic Church
Registration of Inhabitants 81-82
Reichsippenamt 83
Reichsritter (Imperial Knight) 52
Reitstap's Armorial 54
repatriation 11, 44
residents' registers (Einwohnermelde) 81-82
residents' registration office
   (Einwohnermeldeamt) 81-82
"Restoration", BBC programme 48
Reuß (Older and Younger Lines),
   Principalities of 94-95
Rheinland-Pfalz – see Rhineland-
   Palatinate
Rhenish Prussia 93
Rhineland (Rheinland) 21, 63, 93
Rhineland-Palatinate (Rheinland-
   Pfalz) 92, 93
Riemer, Shirley J 58
Ritter, Jürgen 79
Rocker, Rudolph 46
Roman Catholic Archdiocese of
   Vienna (Wien) 97
Roman Catholic Church
   German Roman Catholic Church,
      Whitechapel, – see St
      Boniface,
   Central Archives, Regensburg
      (Bischöflisches Zentralarchiv
      Regensburg) 86, 92
Roman Catholic Churches, London 21
Roman Catholic Diocese of St Pölten,
   Austria 96
Romania – see Siebenbürgen
Rotterdam, the Netherlands 57
Rothschild Family 35

Royal Marines	10, 32-33
Royal Navy	10, 32-33
Rügen, island of	92
Russian Empire	85, 99-101
Russian Poland	101

S

Saarland	93
Sachsen – see Saxony	
Sächsen-Anhalt – see Saxony-Anhalt	
St Boniface, German Roman Catholic Church, Whitechapel	21
St George, German Lutheran Church, Alie Street, London	18-19, 25-26
– see also Ladies Clothing Society	25-26
St James Palace, German Chapel Royal	18, 21-22
St Mark, Fulham	18-22
St Mary in the Savoy (St Marienkirche), London	19, 25
St Paul's German Reformed Church, London	20-21
St Petersburg Archives	100
St Pölten, Roman Catholic Diocese of	96
Sardinian Embassy RC Chapel, London	22
Saxe-Altenburg, Duchy of	94
Saxe-Coburg-Gotha, Duchy of	94
Saxe-Meiningen, Duchy of	94
Saxe-Weimar-Eisenach, Grand Duchy of	94
Saxon Duchies	94-95
Saxony (Sächsen)	93-94
Kingdom of	94
Prussian Province	94
Saxony-Anhalt (Sächsen-Anhalt)	94
Saxony, Lower – see Lower Saxony	
Schlesien – see Silesia	
Schleswig-Holstein	75-76, 94, 99
Genealogy Workgroup (Arbeits-Gruppe Genealogie Schleswig-Holstein e.V. [AGGSHe.V])	75-76
schools, German, in UK	25
Schulze, Rev.	18, 25
Schwarzburg-Rudolstadt, Principality of	94
Schwarzburg-Sonderburg, Principality of	94
Schwerin – see Mecklenburg	
Scotland	14-15, 24
Scottish Record Office, Edinburgh	16
scum boilers	38
Second World War	32-33
Serbia	98
– see also Banat	
– see also Vojvoidina	
ship lists of aliens	37-38
Shorncliffe, Kent	30
Shotley Bridge, County Durham	23
Siebenbürgen	72
Siebmacher, Johann of Nuremburg (d 1610)	53
Siebmacher'schen Wappenbüchern, 1605-1961, General-Index zu den	53-54
Silesia (Schlesien)	87, 94, 101
Slovakia	99
Slovenia (Slowenien)	87, 98
Slowenien – see Slovenia	
Smith, Kenneth L.	70
Society of Friends of Foreigners in Distress	26
Society of Genealogists' Library	8
Solingen	23
South Africa	30-31
South Shields German Church	24
South Tyrol (Südtirol)	23, 87
Staatsarchiv (State Archives)	70
Stadtarchiv (City Archives)	70
Standesamt	63-69

Standesamt I, Berlin 85, 92
Starke Genealogy Index of German
 Nobility 53
"Status Animarum" 96
Sterberegister – see churchbooks
Stettin (Szczecin) 56, 85, 93
Stratford Internment Camp, East
 London 46
Strelitz – see Mecklenburg
Sudetenland 87
Südtirol – see South Tyrol
sugarbakers 20, 22, 38-40, 60
 insurance – see Phoenix Insurance
  Company
 website at **www.mawer.clara.net** 39
Sunderland German Church 24
surnames, German 49-50
 dictionaries 49-50
 feminine suffix -in 49
Swinbank, Christiane 26
Swiss soldiers in British Army 28, 30
Switzerland 101-102
 – citizenship 101-102
 – civil registration 102
swordmakers 23
Sydenham German Evangelical
 Church, London 23
Szczecin – see Stettin

T

tailors 38
Taufregister – see churchbooks
Taylor, Jennifer 48
telephone books (Fernsprechbücher)
 50-51
Theroff, Paul 53
"Three Men on the Bummel" 93
Thüringen – see Thuringia
Thuringia (Thüringen) 94-95
 Reuß (Older and Younger Lines),
  Principalities of 94-95

Saxe-Altenburg, Duchy of 94
Saxe-Coburg-Gotha, Duchy of 94
Saxe-Meiningen, Duchy of 94
Saxe-Weimar-Eisenach, Grand
 Duchy of 94
Saxon Duchies 94-95
Schwarzburg-Rudolstadt,
 Principality of 94
Schwarzburg-Sonderburg,
 Principality of 94
Tower Hamlets Library 20-21
Towey, Jenny 8, 41, 43
Trauregister – see churchbooks
Trebon archives – see Czech Republic
Trepte, August 51
Turkey 44
Tyrol, Italian 23, 87
 – see also South Tyrol

U

UK Border Agency 17
Ukraine 85, 99, 101
Uncapher, Wendy K. 59-60
Upper Austria (Oberösterreich) 96
 Archives (Oberösterreicher
  Landesarchiv) 96
 – see also Abstdorf
USSR (Soviet Union) 92

V

Vienna (Wein) 97-98
 Maria am Gestade 96
 military personnel files for Vienna
  (Grundbuchblätter) 1789-
  1930 97
 Nazi pedigree documents
  (Abstammungsnachweise)
  1938-45 97
 "Our Lady of the Scots" (Unsere
  Liebe Frau zu den Schotten) 96

passport registers (Paßregister)
1792-1918 97
population register cards
(Einwohnermeldezettel)
1850-1920 97
population registers
(Einwohnerkartei) 1700-1950 97
St Rosalia 96
Spital in der Rossau 96
Roman Catholic Archdiocese of,
wills (Testaments) 1548-1850
& estates (Verlaßenschaften)
1789-1850 97
workers' registers
(Arbeiterprotokolle) 1860-
1919 97
Vojvoidina 98
Volksbund Deutsche
Kriegsgräberfursorge e. V. – see
German War Graves Commission
Volkszählungen – see German
Censuses
v. Müthel family 53
Voralberg, Austria 97
archives (Voralberger
Landesarchiv) 97
Vorpommern – see Mecklenburg

W

Waldeckers 28
Wales 14-17, 23
Walling, John 46
Wappen – see German – Coats of
Arms
War Graves Commission – see under
German
wars of unification 90, 91

Warsaw, Grand Duchy of 101
Waterloo, Battle of 30
websites 58-59
Weimar Republic 60
Weiß, Volkmar 73
Wellcome Library 41
Westfalen – see Westphalia
Westphalia (Westfalen) 50, 55, 63,
90, 95
West Prussia (Westpreußen) 87
Weyman family 11, 12, 22, 26, 39
Weymouth, Dorset 30
Whitechapel 19-23
St Mary, Whitechapel 22
Wielkopolska (Greater Poland) – see
also Posen 93
Wikipedia 60
wills 45, 74
proved in Bremen 1599-1890 74
– see also Vienna
Württemberg, Kingdom of 21, 41,
54-55, 95-96
family registers
(Familienregistern) 95-96
– see also pork butchers

Y

Yugoslavia 98-99
– see also Serbia
– see also Slovenia
– see also Vojvoidina

Z

Zanzibar 91
Zoffany, Johann 43